Exploring Literature

Student Workbook

AGS®
American Guidance Service, Inc.
Circle Pines, Minnesota 55014-1796
1-800-328-2560

© 1999 AGS®American Guidance Service, Inc. Circle Pines, MN 55014-1796.

Printed in the United States of America

ISBN 0-7854-1816-4

Product Number 92053

A 0 9 8

Table of Contents

About Fables

Directions On the line, write the letter of the answer that correctly completes each sentence.

1. Fables are usually _____.
   - **a.** short and simple
   - **b.** long and complicated
   - **c.** written in three acts
   - **d.** written with rhyme

2. In fables, the characters are _____.
   - **a.** well-rounded and fully described
   - **b.** not fully described
   - **c.** always animals
   - **d.** always smart

3. The animals in fables often _____.
   - **a.** tell lies
   - **b.** describe their lives with great detail
   - **c.** act like people
   - **d.** become rich

4. Giving animals or objects the characteristics of humans is called _____.
   - **a.** fable
   - **b.** moral
   - **c.** nonfiction
   - **d.** personification

5. We call the characters in fables _____.
   - **a.** flat
   - **b.** well-rounded
   - **c.** complicated
   - **d.** serious

6. Fables usually teach a lesson, or _____ , about life.
   - **a.** personification
   - **b.** fiction
   - **c.** moral
   - **d.** flat

7. The plot, or what happens, in a fable, _____.
   - **a.** is long and complicated
   - **b.** does not take long to unfold
   - **c.** always has three animals, and two humans
   - **d.** has action chases with cars, trains, and helicopters

8. Many Greek fables come from a storyteller whose name was _____.
   - **a.** Alexander
   - **b.** Homer
   - **c.** Aesop
   - **d.** Washington

9. In the beginning, fables were _____.
   - **a.** told only to secret societies
   - **b.** written in large books called testaments
   - **c.** never told to children
   - **d.** not written down

10. Fables are _____.
    - **a.** always written down
    - **b.** nonfiction
    - **c.** fictional stories
    - **d.** biographies

Aesop's Fables

Directions Write *True* if the statement is true; write *False* if the statement is not true. Write your answers on the lines provided before each statement. Make each false statement true by drawing a line through its underlined word. Then write the correct word below the statement.

_____ **1.** The Greek slave <u>Aesop</u> told many fables.

_____

_____ **2.** He was born between 600 and 500 <u>B.C.</u>

_____

_____ **3.** "The Dog and His Reflection" is a <u>poem</u> told by Aesop.

_____

_____ **4.** In this first story, the Dog thinks and behaves like a <u>rabbit</u>.

_____

_____ **5.** The <u>plot</u> of the story is "Being greedy is very foolish."

_____

_____ **6.** Dogs thinking like humans is an example of <u>personification</u>.

_____

_____ **7.** "The Dog in the Manger" was also first told by <u>Lincoln</u>.

_____

_____ **8.** In the second fable, the Dog keeps the Cattle from the <u>barn</u>.

_____

_____ **9.** The <u>moral</u> of the second fable is "Do not keep others from enjoying something you cannot enjoy yourself."

_____

_____ **10.** The main <u>character</u> in both fables is a dog.

_____

More Aesop's Fables

Directions   Circle the word or phrase in parentheses that best completes each set of sentences.

1. The characters in fables are said to be (flat, well-rounded). The author gives the character only a single, important quality and does not develop other traits.

2. The English novelist (William Faulkner, E. M. Forster) first described fable characters this way. Now everyone does.

3. According to one fable, Aesop was the slave of (Alexander, Xanthus). Along with some other slaves, they went on a journey together.

4. Aesop picked the (lightest, heaviest) basket to carry during the long walking trip. The other slaves laughed at him.

5. The basket, however, was the one in which the master had placed the (clothes, food). Thus, it was empty by the end of the trip.

6. In "The Milkmaid and Her Pail," a Milkmaid carries a pail of milk on her head. From the milk, he plans to make (butter, yogurt), which she will sell.

7. The (moral, plot) of "The Milkmaid and Her Pail" is "Do not count your chickens before they hatch." Because the Milkmaid spills her milk, all her plans shatter.

8. In "The North Wind and the Sun," the North Wind and the Sun have a contest. The Sun makes the traveler (take off, put on) his coat.

9. The (North Wind, Sun) wins the contest in the fable "The North Wind and the Sun." The moral of the fable is "You can accomplish more with kindness than you can with force."

10. In fables, (the story, the setting) is more important than the characters. Because the characters are flat, readers find out little about them.

Unit 1
Workbook
4

How the Fly Saved the River

Directions Use the terms in the Word Bank to complete each set of sentences below.

> **Word Bank**
>
> character   moose   hero
> Toronto   North America moral
> Ojibwa   jeer   new
> pesky

1. Ril Gaiashk was born in 1951 in _____, Ontario. He is an Odawa Indian.

2. Aesop told fables about animals in Greece. Gaiashk's fable "How the Fly Saved the River" tells about animals in the northeastern part of _____.

3. The fable comes from the culture of the _____ people. In earlier times, they lived in the forests of eastern Canada.

4. In "How the Fly Saved the River," the fly becomes the _____ of the fable. The fly saves the river for the other animals.

5. The hero of a story or novel is its main _____. In some stories, animals are heroes; in other stories, human beings are heroes.

6. Gaiashk says that this story happened "Many, many years ago when the world was _____." At that time, "there was a beautiful river."

7. All the animals came to drink at the river. But when the big _____ came, he began to drink the river dry.

8. The fly knew how to save the river. But the other animals began to _____ at the tiny creature and make fun of him.

9. Despite this, the fly put his plan in action and bit the big animal all over its body. The fly was so _____ that the moose fled from the river, and didn't come back!

10. The _____ of this fable is "Even the small can fight the strong if they use their brains to think."

The Singing Turtle

Directions Match each item in Column A with its detail or definition in Column B.
Write the letter of each correct answer on the line.

Column A

Column B

_____ 1. Philippe Thoby-Marcelin

_____ 2. Port-au-Prince

_____ 3. "The Singing Turtle"

_____ 4. *waya*

_____ 5. voodoo

_____ 6. setting

_____ 7. millet

_____ 8. Tonton Jean

_____ 9. $200

_____ 10. the king

_____ 11. a turtle

_____ 12. Creole

_____ 13. Sor Mise

_____ 14. the birds

_____ 15. the toad

a. the characters in the Haitian fable whom the turtle is helping work

b. the character who lost a bet in the Haitian fable

c. an example of Haitian dialect

d. a fable or folktale from Haiti

e. a Haitian language based on French

f. a grass grown for grain and used for food

g. a character in the Haitian fable who made a bet with the king

h. the capital of Haiti

i. one of the authors of "The Singing Turtle"

j. the amount of a bet in the Haitian fable

k. the hero of the Haitian fable

l. the time and place of a story

m. the character in the Haitian fable who lets the turtle loose

n. rituals brought to Haiti from Africa

o. the character in the Haitian fable who could not sing for Sor Mise

The King and the Shirt

Directions   Each set of sentences has two missing words. Below each set are three words. Two of these complete the set. Circle the letter of the one word that does not complete the set.

1. Leo Tolstoy is a famous _____ writer. He is best known for his _____ *Anna Karenina* and *War and Peace*.

   a. fables   **b.** novels   **c.** Russian

2. Tolstoy was born in _____. Although famous, he was not happy, and he sold all his property in _____.

   a. 1910   **b.** 1890   **c.** 1828

3. Tolstoy wrote fables for the _____ people of Russia. One of them is "The _____ and the Peas."

   a. young   **b.** Monkey   **c.** Turtle

4. The moral of that fable might be "A _____ in the hand is worth two in the bush." This is like the fable "The _____ and Her Pail."

   a. Milkmaid   **b.** Fly   **c.** bird

5. The "King and the Shirt" is an example of a _____. Tolstoy does not state its _____ or message.

   a. novel   **b.** fable   **c.** moral

6. In "The King and the Shirt," the king becomes _____. He calls all his wise men together to decide how to _____ him.

   a. ill   **b.** homeless   **c.** cure

7. The wise men decide that the king needs the _____ of a happy man. So emissaries go in search of a happy man and find that everyone has something to _____ about.

   a. complain   **b.** shirt   **c.** brag

8. Finally, the king's son passes by a poor _____. He hears a man within praising the great and good _____.

   a. king   **b.** God   **c.** hut

9. When the _____ go inside the hut, the man has no shirt. He is too _____ to have even a shirt, yet he is happy.

   a. poor   **b.** emissaries   **c.** king

10. The ending of this fable is an example of _____. That is, we expect a certain event to take place and the _____ happens.

    a. opposite   **b.** irony   **c.** setting

Unit 1 Review

Part A Directions   Match each item in Column A with its detail or definition in Column B. Write the letter of each correct answer on the line.

Column A

_____ **1.** Aesop

_____ **2.** Greece

_____ **3.** Ril Gaiashk

_____ **4.** Pierre Marcelin

_____ **5.** Toronto, Ontario

_____ **6.** Haiti

_____ **7.** Leo Tolstoy

_____ **8.** Russia

_____ **9.** irony

_____ **10.** fable

_____ **11.** flat

_____ **12.** moral

_____ **13.** setting

_____ **14.** "The Singing Turtle"

_____ **15.** "The Dog in the Manger"

Column B

a. the place and time when a story happens

b. an example of a fable by Aesop

c. a lesson or message about life told in a story

d. the difference between what is expected and what really happens

e. the country in which Pierre Marcelin was born

f. the country in which Leo Tolstoy was born

g. an example of a fable by Pierre Marcelin and Philippe Thoby-Marcelin

h. a story that teaches a lesson about life and often has animals as the characters

i. a word that describes a character who is based on a single quality and is not well developed

j. one of the authors of the fable "The Singing Turtle"

k. a fable writer who is also an Odawa Indian

l. the author of the fable "The King and the Shirt"

m. the country in which Aesop lived

n. the place where Ril Gaiashk was born

o. the slave who wrote fables more than 2,000 years ago

Unit 1 Review, continued

Part B Directions Match the fable title in Column C with its moral in Column D.
Write the letter of each correct answer on the line.

Column C

_____ **1.** "The Dog and His Reflection"

_____ **2.** "The Dog in the Manger"

_____ **3.** "The Milkmaid and Her Pail"

_____ **4.** "The North Wind and the Sun"

_____ **5.** "How the Fly Saved the River"

Column D

a. Do not keep others from enjoying something you cannot enjoy yourself.

b. You can accomplish more with kindness than you can with force.

c. Being greedy is very foolish.

d. Even the small can fight the strong if they use their brains to think.

e. Do not count your chickens before they hatch.

About Myths

Directions Use the terms in the Word Bank to complete each set of sentences below.

Word Bank			
characters	India	oral	Zeus
creation	myths	religious	Hopi
nature	Thor		

1. People from every culture have created _____. These explain what they did not understand about the creation of the world and nature.

2. Like fables, myths were first _____. That is, people told them to one another for many years before writing them down.

3. The _____ in these myths were gods, goddesses, and strong heroes. We find out more about them than the ones we meet in fables.

4. Myths were part of people's _____ belief. They believed in the power of many gods and goddesses.

5. One group of myths explains how the world and all its creatures came into being. We call these _____ myths.

6. A myth of the _____ Indians says that all living things came from deep within the earth. In a Polynesian myth, two parents bring life to earth.

7. A creation myth from _____ tells of an animal that dove deep into the sea. It brought up a small piece of earth that grew into our world.

8. Another type of myth explains events in _____, such as thunderstorms. People are less afraid when they have reasons for things.

9. The god _____ created thunder and lightning by throwing a hammer at his enemies. This is a Norse myth.

10. The Greeks believed that thunderbolts were the weapons of _____, the king of their gods. Thunderstorms were the Greek gods fighting among themselves.

Prometheus

Directions Write *True* if the statement is true; write *False* if the statement is
not true. Write your answers on the lines provided before each statement.
Make each false statement true by drawing a line through its underlined
word. Then write the correct word below the statement.

_____ **1.** The group of giant gods were known as <u>Titans</u>.

_____

_____ **2.** Prometheus and Epimetheus were twin <u>sisters</u>.

_____

_____ **3.** Epimetheus gave all the best gifts of the gods to <u>animals</u>.

_____

_____ **4.** Prometheus decided to give humans the gift of <u>money</u>.

_____

_____ **5.** Fire was a gift that only the <u>gods</u> enjoyed.

_____

_____ **6.** But Prometheus sneaked into <u>Olympus</u> and lit a torch from
the god's fire and carried it to earth.

_____

_____ **7.** Zeus punished Prometheus by chaining him to a <u>boat</u>.

_____

_____ **8.** For 30,000 years, a giant <u>lizard</u> ate from his liver each day.

_____

_____ **9.** <u>Thor</u> sent Hercules to kill the eagle and release Prometheus.

_____

_____ **10.** But <u>Hercules</u> always had to carry a piece of the rock to which
he had been chained and a link of the chain.

_____

Demeter and Persephone

Part A Directions Match each item in Column A with its detail or definition in Column B. Write the letter of each correct answer on the line.

Column A

_____ **1.** Demeter

_____ **2.** Gaea

_____ **3.** gardener

_____ **4.** Hades

_____ **5.** Helios

_____ **6.** Persephone

_____ **7.** pomegranate

_____ **8.** Rhea

_____ **9.** winter

_____ **10.** Zeus

Column B

a. food of the dead

b. the king of the Greek gods

c. the earth mother

d. the harvest goddess

e. the daughter of Demeter

f. the god of the underworld

g. the one who showed Hades the pomegranate

h. he season when Persephone is in the underworld

i. the oldest and most respected goddess

j. the sun god

Part B Directions Read each sentence. Write *T* if the statement is true or *F* if it is not true.

_____ **1.** The myth of Demeter and Persephone explains the seasons.

_____ **2.** Hades stole Demeter and took her to the underworld.

_____ **3.** Demeter cursed the earth and the crops failed to grow.

_____ **4.** Zeus ordered Rhea to return Persephone to Demeter.

_____ **5.** In winter, Persephone is in the underworld with Hades.

Perseus and Medusa

Directions On the line, write the letter of the answer that correctly completes each sentence.

1. Perseus, a great hero, decided to kill _____.

   a. the Gorgon Medusa   **b.** Zeus   **c.** Hermes   **d.** Persephone

2. The Gorgons had hair that was a mass of squirming _____.

   a. cats   **b.** worms   **c.** snakes   **d.** branches

3. One glance from a Gorgon would turn Perseus to _____.

   a. ashes   **b.** stone   **c.** slime   **d.** soot

4. The god Hermes gave Perseus the gift of winged _____.

   a. ears   **b.** sandals   **c.** eagles   **d.** capes

5. The goddess Athena gave Perseus the gift of a gleaming _____ .

   a. shield   **b.** sword   **c.** teakettle   **d.** diamond

6. Perseus also needed magical gifts from the _____.

   a. Grey Women   **b.** Gorgons   **c.** Greeks   **d.** Nymphs of the North

7. To find them, Perseus went to the _____ Women who could tell him where the Nymphs of the North lived.

   a. Old   **b.** Young   **c.** Grey   **d.** Lonely

8. The Nymphs of the North gave him the Cap of _____.

   a. Light   **b.** Darkness   **c.** Night   **d.** Day

9. With this gift, Perseus would be _____ to Medusa.

   a. kind   **b.** invisible   **c.** interesting   **d.** visible

10. Perseus cut off Medusa's head and put it in the magic _____, which the Nymphs of the North had given him.

    a. sea   **b.** bag   **c.** oven   **d.** box

The Beginning and the End of the World

Directions   Each set of sentences has two missing words. Below each set are
three words. Two of these complete the set. Circle the letter of the
one word that does not complete the set.

1. "The Beginning and the End of the World" is a _____ myth. It comes from the _____
    people of the Pacific Northwest.

    a. fable   **b.** creation   **c.** Okanogan

2. According to the myth, this happened long ago, when the sun was _____. In the middle
    of the ocean was an _____.

    a. island   **b.** young   **c.** old

3. The _____ was called Samah-tumi-whoo-lah. On it lived a race of _____.

    a. island   **b.** ocean   **c.** giants

4. The ruler of this island was _____. She had _____ powers and could create whatever
    she wished.

    a. Tahmahnawis   **b.** Okanogan   **c.** Scomalt

5. The white giants began to _____, so the leader drove them to the end of the island. Then
    she pushed that end out to _____.

    a. sea   **b.** cry   **c.** quarrel

6. All the people died except one man and one woman. The man caught a _____. When their
    island sank, they built a _____.

    a. raft   **b.** canoe   **c.** whale

7. They paddled until they came to some _____. At last they reached the mainland and _____.

    a. cities   **b.** islands   **c.** stopped

8. They wandered toward the _____ and came to where they wanted to stay. The Indians
    now call this _____ country.

    a. sunrise   **b.** Okanogan   **c.** Scomalt

9. By now their _____ was gone for the sun had burned their skin. Now they were
    reddish _____.

    a. blueness   **b.** brown   **c.** whiteness

10. At a future time, the Okanogan Indians say, the _____ will melt the world's foundations.
    The _____ will cut the world loose.

    a. lakes   **b.** rivers   **c.** islands

Loki and the Master Builder

Directions Circle the word in parentheses that best completes each set of sentences.

1. Snorri Sturluson was one of the first people to collect the (oral, few) Norse myths into a written work. He was born in 1179.

2. Sturluson was born in (Iceland, Newfoundland), where the Norse people settled. The king of Norway feared him, however, and had him killed.

3. "Loki and the Master Builder" shows how powerful the (Norse, Greek) gods were. Loki is a giant who lives among the gods.

4. In this myth, a master builder offers to build a stronghold for the gods. As his reward, he wants Freyja, the goddess of fertility, death, love, and (thunder, war).

5. The gods agree; however, the master builder has to build the stronghold in one (summer, winter). If he does not, the gods will not pay him.

6. The master builder asks the gods to let him use his (ox, horse), Svadilfari. Loki advises the gods to grant this wish to the builder.

7. The builder uses huge (boulders, beams) to build the stronghold. By three days before summer, the work on it is almost finished.

8. That same evening, Loki turned himself into a (horse, wind). The builder's horse followed Loki into the woods and delayed the work on the stronghold.

9. The master builder had asked for Freyja and the sun and the (stars, moon). But he receives only death in payment for all his work.

10. (Thor, Zeus) raises his hammer and kills the master builder. He sends him tumbling down to Niflhel.

The Moon Spirit and Coyote Woman

Part A Directions   Write *True* if the set of sentences is true; write *False* if the set is not true. Write your answers on the lines provided before each set of sentences. Make each false set true by drawing a line through its underlined word. Then write the correct word below the set.

_____   **1.** Clive Grace is a qualified <u>storyteller</u> in Great Britain. He lives in Bath, England, with his dog, Galen.

_____

_____   **2.** His story "The Moon Spirit and Coyote Woman" is a <u>fable</u>. Grace created this story to tell orally.

_____

_____   **3.** In it, the <u>wolf</u> Tanais tells a story-within-a-story. That is, he tells a second story within the first story about him.

_____

_____   **4.** Tanais tells the <u>sun</u> a story that happened long ago. It is a story about the first creatures to be made for the new land.

_____

_____   **5.** In his story, he says that some believe the <u>coyote</u> was the first creature to be made for Earth. Now Tanais begins his story.

_____

_____   **6.** Coyote Woman was a beloved medicine woman. Her favorite place was a rocky <u>cove</u>.

_____

_____   **7.** In a pool of water, she saw the face of a <u>star</u> spirit. The spirit pulled himself out of the water, and they fell in love.

_____

The Moon Spirit and Coyote Woman, continued

_____ **8.** Coyote Woman and <u>Star</u> Coyote married and found happiness together for a short time. One day he went on a hunt.

_____

_____ **9.** A herd of <u>horses</u> trampled Coyote Woman's husband. He died, and she grieved deeply for him.

_____

_____ **10.** Tanais says that some stories say that Coyote Woman died too, of a broken <u>back</u>. She is now a star in the sky.

_____

Part B Directions   Match each item in Column A with its detail or definition in Column B. Write the letter of each correct answer on the line.

Column A

Column B

_____ **1.** Tanais

_____ **2.** Coyote Woman

_____ **3.** Moon Coyote

_____ **4.** Galen

_____ **5.** Clive Grace

a. a fox who tells a story about coyotes

b. the author of the myth about coyotes

c. a medicine woman

d. the dog who lives with the author of this myth

e. the husband of Coyote Woman

Unit 2 Review

Part A Directions   Match each cause in Column A with its result, or effect, in Column B. Write the letter of each correct answer on the line. Remember that a cause is something that makes a result, or an effect, happen.

Column A

_____ **1.** Epimetheus gives all the special gifts of the gods to animals

_____ **2.** Zeus feels that Prometheus has tricked him.

_____ **3.** Zeus gives Hercules a special task.

_____ **4.** Hades kidnaps Persephone.

_____ **5.** Persephone eats seeds from the pomegranate.

_____ **6.** Persephone has to return to Hades for part of the year.

_____ **7.** Polydectes does not tell Perseus to bring a gift to the wedding.

_____ **8.** Perseus captures the one eye shared by the Grey Women.

_____ **9.** Perseus puts on his cap of invisibility.

_____ **10.** Perseus looks into the shield Athena had given him.

Column B

a. So Demeter makes all the crops wither and die.

b. So the Grey Women tell Perseus where the Nymphs of the North live.

c. So the Gorgons cannot see Perseus coming.

d. So no special gifts are left for Prometheus to give to human beings.

e. So Medusa's gaze does not turn Perseus to stone.

f. So Demeter causes the crops to die again, and Earth endures winter.

g. So Zeus has Prometheus chained to a rock and has an eagle eat from his liver each day.

h. So Persephone has to return to the underground for part of the year.

i. So Perseus decides to bring the king the head of the Gorgon Medusa.

j. So Hercules shoots the eagle with a special arrow and releases Prometheus from his chains.

Unit 2 Review, continued

Part B Directions Match each cause in Column C with its result, or effect, in Column D. Write the letter of each correct answer on the line. Remember that a cause is something that makes a result, or an effect, happen.

Column C

_____ 1. The white giants begin to war with one another and kill people.

_____ 2. The white giants gather in one place on the island.

_____ 3. The floating island begins to sink.

_____ 4. A master builder offers to make a strong-hold for the Norse gods and demands that Freyja be his payment.

_____ 5. By three days before summer, the master builder's work is almost finished.

_____ 6. Loki turns himself into a mare.

_____ 7. Tanais sees the moon's reflection in the sea.

_____ 8. Coyote Woman falls in love with the face in the pool of water.

_____ 9. Moon Coyote has never hunted before and he miscalculates as he chases after his prey.

_____ 10. Her heart broken, Coyote Woman dies too.

Column D

a. So Scomalt breaks off that piece of the island and pushes it out to sea.

b. So the master builder's stallion runs into the woods after the mare.

c. So the Norse gods give the builder only one winter to build the stronghold.

d. So the fox begins to tell the moon a story about coyotes.

e. So Scomalt drives the white giants to one end of the island.

f. So Moon Coyote lifts himself out of the pool of water.

g. So the man and the woman build a canoe.

h. So two stars seem joined together as one in the sky.

i. So the Norse gods begin to worry that they might have to give Freyja as payment.

j. So Moon Coyote is trampled when the buffalo herd swerves madly.

About Tall Tales and Legends

Directions   Circle the term in parentheses that best completes each set of sentences.

1. (Folklore, Nonfiction) includes stories and fairy tales, as well as sayings, games, songs, and dances. People preserve their history through this type of literature.

2. One important part of American folklore is the (tall tale, obituary). People from many different cultures brought their folklore with them to America.

3. For instance, stories in (German, African) folklore told about the adventures of a Trickster Rabbit who could outsmart his enemies. In America, this character became B'rer Rabbit, a hero of many American folktales.

4. Folklore first began as (oral, written) literature. That is, most tall tales and legends, like fables and myths, were first passed along by word of mouth.

5. Tall tales have plot, characters, and settings. In America, the setting is often the (frontier, ocean), and the characters are often pioneers.

6. The characters in tall tales tend to be taller, stronger, smarter, and braver than the usual person. For instance, Pecos Bill rode a (cyclone, evergreen tree) and created Death Valley.

7. A second type of folklore is the (ballet, legend). These stories tell about real people, places, or events.

8. In legends, the characters are people who actually lived, such as Daniel Boone and (B'rer Rabbit, Davy Crockett), or who may have actually lived, such as John Henry. Other legends are built around a real event or a real place.

9. American folklore gives us a chance to look (back, forward) to our past. These stories help us appreciate the great variety of cultures that went into the settling of our country.

10. In legends, some details are historically true. However, other details come straight from the storyteller's (history books, imagination).

Babe the Blue Ox

Directions   Write *True* if the statement is true; write *False* if the statement is not true. Write your answers on the lines provided before each statement. Make each false statement true by drawing a line through its underlined word. Then write the correct word below the statement.

_____   **1.** The imaginary folk hero Paul Bunyan was a huge <u>lumberjack</u>.

            _____

_____   **2.** Paul's sidekick was Babe, a <u>blue</u> ox.

            _____

_____   **3.** When Babe was a calf, his color was <u>red</u>.

            _____

_____   **4.** Once Babe pulled the crooks out of <u>18</u> miles of a road.

            _____

_____   **5.** Brimstone <u>Ned</u> took care of Babe.

            _____

_____   **6.** Babe ate <u>4</u> tons of grain at a single meal and who knows how much hay.

            _____

_____   **7.** One logger in the lumbering camp compared the amount of Babe's manure to that of the Augean stables, which the <u>Norse</u> hero "Herukles" cleaned out.

            _____

_____   **8.** When Brimstone heard this comparison, he got <u>angry</u>.

            _____

_____   **9.** At one point, Paul bought a <u>soybean</u> farm down in Wisconsin and this made feeding Babe easier for Brimstone.

            _____

_____   **10.** Paul Bunyan used to say to Babe, "Be <u>happy</u>."

            _____

Feboldson, Western Scientist

Directions Match each cause in Column A with its result, or effect in Column B.
Write the letter of each correct answer on the line. Remember that a
cause is something that makes a result, or an effect, happen.

Column A

_____ 1. Wherever he went, Walter Blair collected stories.

_____ 2. Hunks of Nebraska became other s tates, containing mountains.

_____ 3. The Great Heat made Nebraska devilish hot.

_____ 4. One day Febold looked at the sky and decided fog was coming.

_____ 5. London has thicker fogs than anywhere else except on the ocean.

_____ 6. Febold saw a dark gray thing, no bigger than a hand, in the sky.

_____ 7. For forty days and nights, Nebraskans heard a hissing noise.

_____ 8. Ten miles up in the sky the rain was spattering down on hot air.

_____ 9. As the steam, made from rain, hissed, it became fog.

_____ 10. Soon, walking alone became impossible.

_____ 11. Cattle could drink the fog.

_____ 12. The seeds figured that the closest sunshine was in China.

_____ 13. The fog-cutters arrived from London.

_____ 14. Febold cut the fog into big, neat strips.

_____ 15. Febold put the fog strips along the dirt roads of Nebraska.

Column B

a. So the mercury in thermometers shot up the tubes and spewed out the top like a fountain.

b. So London inventors had the opportunity to invent the best fog-cutters.

c. So when he went to graduate school, all these stories went with him.

d. So soon he had great piles of strips and had to put them somewhere.

e. So when the rain hit the hot air, steam developed and made a hissing noise.

f. So the farmers did not need to water their cattle.

g. So the seeds started growing downward.

h. So the whole of Nebraska was nothing but valleys, tableland, and rolling prairies.

i. So Febold first used the fog-cutters to cut the red tape.

j. So fog began to hover over the ground.

k. So in spring, the old fog seeps up on the dirt roads, turning them into goo.

l. So Febold concluded that rain would break the heat and bring fog.

m. So the people in Nebraska went nearly crazy.

n. So two people needed to walk together, one parting the fog, the other walking through.

o. So he ordered fog cutters from London, England.

John Henry

Directions On the line, write the letter of the answer that correctly completes each sentence.

1. When John Henry was a baby, he picked up a _____.

    a. rock   **b.** toy
    c. hammer   **d.** firecracker

2. John Henry was a man _____ feet high.

    a. four   **b.** five
    c. six   **d.** seven

3. As a man, John Henry first used a hammer that weighed _____ pounds.

    a. nine   **b.** fifteen
    c. twenty   **d.** thirty

4. When the railroad came to a tall _____, John Henry knew he would need a bigger hammer.

    a. skyscraper   **b.** mountain
    c. overpass   **d.** evergreen tree

5. Now, John Henry asked his boss for a _____ -pound hammer.

    a. ten   **b.** twelve
    c. thirty   **d.** forty

6. John Henry was in a contest with a _____.

    a. steam drill   **b.** woman from the West
    c. Nebraska scientist   **d.** giant from the North Woods

7. With his hammer, John Henry sunk the steel down _____ feet.

    a. ten   **b.** twelve
    c. fourteen   **d.** sixteen

8. The steam drill sunk the steel down only _____ feet.

    a. six   **b.** nine
    c. twelve   **d.** fifteen

9. John Henry hammered on the _____ -hand side.

    a. left   **b.** top
    c. bottom   **d.** right

10. John Henry beat the steam drill, but in doing so, he _____.

    a. broke his hammer   **b.** hammered his heart to death
    c. got a knot in his arm   **d.** hit his foot and broke the bones

Life and Adventures of Calamity Jane, by Herself

Part A Directions   Place each event in its correct order. Write the letter of the first event from Calamity Jane's story after #1. Write the letter of the second event from the story after #2 and so on. Note that #10 will be the last event.

Events in Order

#1. _____

#2. _____

#3. _____

#4. _____

#5. _____

#6. _____

#7. _____

#8. _____

#9. _____

#10. _____

List of Events to Be Put in Order

a.   Jane's mother died in Black Foot, Montana, in 1866.

b.   During campaign of 1872–73, Jane is given her name "Calamity."

c.   In 1884, Jane goes to San Francisco.

d.   Jane lived in Deadwood where her friend Wild Bill Hickock was murdered in August 1876.

e.   Jane left Deadwood and moved to Yellow Stone where she ran a wayside inn until 1883.

f.   Jane married Mr. Clinton Burk of Texas in 1885.

g.   Jane became a scout in the winter of 1871.

h.   Jane became a member of the Wild West shows in 1896.

i.   After Hickock's death, Jane left Deadwood one day and rescued the six passengers on the overland mail running from Cheyenne to Deadwood.

j.   Jane stayed with her father until his death in Utah in 1867.

Life and Adventures of Calamity Jane, by Herself, continued

Part B Directions   Match each item in Column C with its detail or definition in Column D. Write the letter of each correct answer on the line.

Column C

_____ **1.** Deadwood, South Dakota

_____ **2.** Marthy Cannary Burk

_____ **3.** Wild Bill Hickock

_____ **4.** Princeton, Missouri

_____ **5.** Virginia City, Montana

_____ **6.** Sheridan, Wyoming

_____ **7.** Fort Meade

_____ **8.** El Paso, Texas

_____ **9.** Boulder, Colorado

_____ **10.** Minneapolis, Minnesota

Column D

a. the place where Calamity Jane was born in 1852

b. the town that is located where Jane saved Captain Egan and was named "Calamity"

c. the town in which Calamity Jane appeared in 1876, dressed in men's clothes

d. a friend of Jane's who was murdered in Deadwood

e. the place where Jane married her husband

f. a fort built by Jane and the 7th U. S. Cavalry

g. the first place where Jane appeared in a Wild West show

h. the town to which Jane's family emigrated in 1865 from Missouri

i. the place where Jane and her husband and daughter set up a hotel

j. the real name of Calamity Jane

The Phantom Hitchhiker

Directions   Use the terms in the Word Bank to complete each set of
sentences below.

Word Bank		
Cohen	Harris	magazine
robe	Chicago	jacket
Middletown	dress	Kearns
Oaklawn		

1. The author of this modern American legend is Daniel _____. He was born in 1936 and writes mostly about ghosts.

2. The author was born in _____. He and his wife work together and now live in New Jersey.

3. The author is a former managing editor of *Science Digest* _____. And he had written a number of science books.

4. The first character we meet in "The Phantom Hitchhiker" is Joel _____. He has been driving for twenty-one hours and admits to having pushed himself too hard.

5. The driver meets a young girl on the road. She is wearing a flimsy _____, and the rain is coming down hard.

6. She says that she lives in_____. The driver is going there too and says he will take her to her home.

7. The girl begins to shiver so the driver turns up the heat. Then he gives her a _____ to put on.

8. When they arrive at her home, the driver looks in the backseat and discovers the girl has disappeared. Confused, he knocks on the door and a woman greets him, dressed in a _____.

9. The mother says that her daughter had been killed ten years before in an automobile accident on the road the driver had driven on. The girl's name is Laura _____.

10. The next day, the driver goes to _____ Cemetery and sees Laura's tombstone. Draped over it is his jacket.

Unit 3 Review

Part A Directions Match each story in Column A with one of its setting in
Column B. Write the letter of each correct answer on the line.

Column A

_____ **1.** "Babe the Blue Ox"

_____ **2.** "Feboldson, Western Scientist"

_____ **3.** "John Henry"

_____ **4.** "Life and Adventures of
Calamity Jane, by Herself"

_____ **5.** "The Phantom Hitchhiker"

Column B

a. "The whole of Nebraska was nothing but valleys, tableland and rolling prairies, all with a southwestern exposure."

b. "I had gone about twelve miles from Deadwood, at the mouth of Whitewood creek, when I met the overland mail running from Cheyenne to Deadwood."

c. "We was all sittin' around the stove that night spinnin' yarns like we almost always done of an evenin' while our socks was dryin.'"

d. "It was the worst house on a bad street. In fact, the house was so dilapidated that it looked deserted."

e. "They laid his body in the sand./Now every woman riding on a C and O train/Says, 'There lies my steel-driving man, Lord, Lord,/There lies my steel-driving man.'"

Unit 3 Review, continued

Part B Directions   Match each tall tale or legend in Column C with three of its characters from Column D.

Column C

_____ **1.** "Babe the Blue Ox"

_____ **2.** "Feboldson, Western Scientist"

_____ **3.** "John Henry"

_____ **4.** "Life and Adventures of Calamity Jane, by Herself"

_____ **5.** "The Phantom Hitchhiker"

Column D

a. Joel Harris, Mrs. Kearns, Laura Kearns

b. Febold, his wife, a fellow in Saline County

c. Wild Bill Hickock, Captain Egan, Clinton Burk

d. Paul Bunyan, Brimstone Bill, Ole

e. a boss or captain, a shaker, and a mama

Part C Directions   Match each tall tale or legend in Column E with three objects, or props, from the story in Column F.

Column E

_____ **1.** "Babe the Blue Ox"

_____ **2.** "Feboldson, Western Scientist"

_____ **3.** "John Henry"

_____ **4.** "Life and Adventures of Calamity Jane, by Herself"

_____ **5.** "The Phantom Hitchhiker"

Column F

a. horses, guns, men's clothing

b. a yoke, grain, hay

c. fog-cutters, thermometers, barometers

d. tombstone, car, jacket

e. hammer, steam drill, piece of steel

Part D Directions   On the blank lines, write a title from Unit 3 for each item. Note that you may use some titles more than once.

1. Name one folklore story from Unit 3. _____

2. Name one tall tale from Unit 3. _____

3. Name one legend from Unit 3. _____

4. Name one ballad from Unit 3. _____

5. Name one modern urban legend from Unit 3. _____

About the Short Story

Directions Use the terms in the Word Bank to complete each set of sentences below.

WordBank		
antagonist	fiction	novels
poetry	protagonist	characters
narrator	paragraphs	prose
short		

1. We call brief works of fiction _____ stories. They first appeared in the nineteenth century and were written by Poe, Hawthorne, and Irving.

2. This type of fiction has fewer _____ than novels do. These may be people or animals.

3. The main character in a piece of fiction is the _____ . Another word for this character is the hero.

4. Another character in a piece of fiction is the _____. This character is a person or force that tries to keep the hero from accomplishing his or her goal.

5. A _____ tells the story. If his or her point of view is from inside the story, then we have the first-person point of view.

6. Short stories are _____; that is, they did not actually happen. Authors may base their plot and characters on actual events and people, but they change these to serve the needs of the story.

7. Short stories belong to the kind of literature known as _____. It uses words that sound like ordinary language.

8. Another kind of literature is _____. It includes all forms of writing that use special patterns of words and rhythm.

9. Some people think of prose as writing that is organized into _____. The number of them varies in each piece of prose.

10. We use the term _____ to describe longer pieces of fiction that have a more complicated plot. Generally, they have more characters, conflict, and details than short stories.

The Celebrated Jumping Frog of Calaveras County

Part A Directions   Unscramble the word groups below to make a true statement.
On the line, write the four letters of the statement in their correct order.

1. **a.** and met a talkative old man
    b. the narrator of the story
    c. in a California mining town
    d. went to a tavern located   _____

2. **a.** Simon Wheeler told the narrator
    b. who bet on anything that turned up
    c. a story about Jim Smiley
    d. and was very lucky   _____

3. **a.** would take so many days
    b. to get to where he was going
    c. Smiley would bet that a straddle-bug
    d. and Smiley would follow the bug to be sure _____

4. **a.** that the other miners called
    b. but she always won her races
    c. a fifteen-minute nag
    d. Smiley had a mare   _____

5. **a.** he also had a dog
    b. and who grabbed hold of a dog's hind leg
    c. whose name was Andrew Jackson
    d. and seemed frozen to it   _____

6. **a.** so Andrew lost his owner's bet
    b. Andrew Jackson once fought
    c. and went off and died
    d. a dog that had no hind leg   _____

7. **a.** whose name was Dan'l Webster
    b. and catch flies
    c. to jump on a dead level
    d. Jim Smiley taught a frog   _____

8. **a.** Smiley bet with a stranger
    b. who put quail shot in Dan'l Webster
    c. and so the frog lost the bet
    d. and then Smiley got mad.   _____

The Celebrated Jumping Frog of Calaveras County, continued

Part B Directions   Complete the crossword puzzle by using the twelve words in the Word Bank.

Across

3. Mark Twain got his writing, or pen, name in South _____.

7. This story takes place in a mining town in the state of _____.

9. The legendary hero of the story is Jim _____, who bet on a horse, a dog, and a jumping frog.

10. The man who told the story to the narrator was Simon _____.

11. The name of the jumping frog was Dan'l _____.

Down

1. One of Twain's most famous books is *Huckleberry* _____.

2. In this story, Twain uses _____, or exaggerated character descriptions.

4. Mark Twain was born in the state of _____.

5. Another of his famous books is *Tom* _____.

6. The author of this short story is Mark _____.

7. The name he was born with was Samuel Langhorne _____.

8. The name of Jim Smiley's dog was _____ Jackson.

Word Bank

America	caricature
Missouri	Twain
Andrew	Clemens
Sawyer	Webster
California	*Finn*
Smiley	Wheeler

Everyday Use

Part A Directions   Match each item in Column A with its defining word or phrase in Column B. Write the letter of the correct answer on the line.

Column A   **Column B**

_____ **1.** Augusta   **a.** the name of the narrator of the story

_____ **2.** Dee   **b.** the name of the man Maggie will probably marry

_____ **3.** Dicie   **c.** the name of the man Dee lives with

_____ **4.** Georgia   **d.** the name of the sister who is visiting the narrator

_____ **5.** Hakim-a-barber   **e.** the name of the sister who has been burnt and lives with the narrator

_____ **6.** John Thomas   **f.** the name of the aunt after whom Dee has been named

_____ **7.** Maggie   **g.** the last name of the author of this short story

_____ **8.** Mama   **h.** the state in which the author was born

_____ **9.** Walker   **i.** the African name Dee has taken

_____ **10.** Wangero   **j.** the name of the city where Dee went to college

Part B Directions   Read each sentence. Write *T* if the statement is true or *F* if it is not true.

_____ **1.** In this story, the mother's quilts become symbols.

_____ **2.** At the end of the story, Dee takes home the two quilts that the narrator had promised to give to Maggie.

_____ **3.** Maggie was burned in a fire at school.

_____ **4.** For her visit, Dee wears a bright dress that goes down to the ground.

_____ **5.** In the story, Dee starts collecting things to take to her own home.

American History

Part A Directions Write *True* if the statement is true; write *False* if the statement is not true. Write your answers on the lines provided before each statement. Make each false statement true by drawing a line through its underlined word. Then write the correct word below the statement.

_____ **1.** The author of "American History" is <u>Judith</u> Ortiz-Cofer.

_____

_____ **2.** The story is about Elena, a Puerto Rican girl living in a rundown part of a <u>Wyoming</u> city.

_____

_____ **3.** The Puerto Ricans Elena knows think that President <u>Johnson</u> is a saint.

_____

_____ **4.** When Elena plays <u>jump rope</u> with her classmates, they abuse her.

_____

_____ **5.** The one light in Elena's life is <u>Eugene</u>, a boy at school.

_____

_____ **6.** Each evening, she watches him from the <u>back porch</u> of her tenement building.

_____

_____ **7.** He is new to the neighborhood, and Elena introduces herself to him one day <u>before</u> school.

_____

_____ **8.** He helps Elena think of the <u>present</u> rather than the future.

_____

_____ **9.** The story reaches its climax, or high point, on the day that President <u>Kennedy</u> is assassinated

_____

_____ **10.** Elena meets her friend's <u>father</u>, who tells her to go home.

_____

American History, continued

Part B Directions   Match each cause in Column A with its result, or effect in Column B. Write the letter of each correct answer on the line. Remember that a cause is something that makes a result, or an effect, happen.

Column A

_____ **1.** Elena's mother was unhappy in Paterson, New Jersey.

_____ **2.** Ever since moving into El Building, Elena watched the people next door from a place on the fire escape.

_____ **3.** The girls at school abused Elena at school.

_____ **4.** The old man next door died, and his wife moved away.

_____ **5.** Eugene spoke good English, but English was not Elena's first language.

_____ **6.** Elena did not tell Eugene that she could see inside his kitchen from her fire escape.

_____ **7.** Eugene became the one bright light in Elena's world.

_____ **8.** Her mother saw that Elena was infatuated.

_____ **9.** One day, President Kennedy was assassinated.

_____ **10.** That day, Elena knocked at Eugene's door, hoping to visit.

Column B

a. So in August, Eugene and his family moved into the house.

b. So she felt dishonest, but she liked her secret sharing of his evenings.

c. So she wanted to move to Passaic where Elena's father worked.

d. So she came into Elena's room and talked to her about virtue and morality.

e. So she ended up being disappointed because his mother answered and told Elena to go home.

f. So she felt nervous when they played jump rope on the playground.

g. So Mr. DePalma, the P. E. coach, dismissed the students early.

h. So she began to act infatuated with him.

i. So she knew a great deal about the Jewish couple who lived there.

j. So they were not in the same classes at school.

Thank You, M'am

Directions   Match the sentence beginnings in Column A with the sentence endings in Column B. By doing this, create a true sentence about this short story. Write the letter of the correct answer on the line.

Column A

_____ 1. Langston Hughes was born in Joplin, Missouri . . .

_____ 2. His short story "Thank You, M'am," . . .

_____ 3. In the story, Roger tries to steal a woman's purse, . . .

_____ 4. She tells him to pick up her purse, . . .

_____ 5. The woman says her name is . . .

_____ 6. Mrs. Jones drags Roger to her nearby door, . . .

_____ 7. In the kitchenette, she . . .

_____ 8. After he gives his name, . . .

_____ 9. Mrs. Jones says that Roger must have tried to steal her purse because . . .

_____ 10. But Roger says that he wants . . .

_____ 11. Mrs. Jones says that Roger does not need to steal, all he has to do is . .

_____ 12. Mrs. Jones says that all people have . . .

_____ 13. Mrs. Jones goes behind a screen, . . .

_____ 14. Roger offers . . .

_____ 15. After Mrs. Jones feeds him, Roger leaves and tries to say, . . .

Column B

a. . . . but she grabs hold of him and shakes him.

b. . . . he was hungry.

c. . . . Mrs. Luella Bates Washington Jones.

d. . . . to buy a pair of blue suede shoes.

e. . . . she tells him to go and wash his face.

f. . . . and she bends down so he can do so.

g. . . . but later moved to New York City to go to college there.

h. . . . demands to know Roger's name.

i. . . . down the hall, and into the kitchenette at the rear of the house.

j. . . . is brief, even for a short story, so we call it sudden fiction.

k. . . . "Thank you, M'am."

l. . . . done things that they would not want to tell God about.

m. . . . to go to the store for Mrs. Jones

n. . . . but Roger doesn't run away.

o. . . . ask her for money.

Unfinished Message

Directions Place each event in its correct order. Write the letter of the first event
from "Unfinished Message" after #1. Write the letter of the second event
from the story after #2 and so on. Note that #15 will be the last event.

Events in Order

#1. _____

#2. _____

#3. _____

#4. _____

#5. _____

#6. _____

#7. _____

#8. _____

#9. _____

#10. _____

#11. _____

#12. _____

#13. _____

#14. _____

#15. _____

List of Events to Be Put in Order

a. Before the story begins, the United States enters World War II.

b. The narrator and his mother receive word that Kazuo is coming back on a hospital ship.

c. The narrator and his mother visit the DeWitt Army Hospital in Auburn, California, and see Kazuo.

d. Before the story begins, the narrator's family is forced to move to the Relocation Center in Utah.

e. The narrator and his mother take two weeks to clean their California house.

f. The narrator and his mother receive a wire from the War Department that Kazuo has been seriously wounded on May 5, 1945.

g. The narrator and his mother return to California.

h. The mother dies in her sleep on August 5, 1946.

i. On May 5, 1945, the narrator's mother cannot sleep because she keeps seeing her son Kazuo's face.

j. The army transfers Kazuo to Letterman Hospital in San Francisco, California.

k. Kazuo returns to their California home in a wheelchair.

l. The narrator touches the window and recalls his mother's words: "I can't stop worrying over you, my son."

m. The narrator hears a slight tapping on the window.

n. Kazuo tells his brother that he has heard a tapping too.

o. Kazuo raises a family in San Leandro, California.

Unit 4 Review

Part A Directions   Match each character's name in Column A with his or her description in Column B. Write the letter of each correct answer on the line.

Column A

_____ **1.** Simon Wheeler

_____ **2.** Jim Smiley

_____ **3.** Mama in "Everyday Use"

_____ **4.** Maggie

_____ **5.** Dee

_____ **6.** Hakim-a-barber

_____ **7.** John Thomas

_____ **8.** Elena

_____ **9.** Eugene

_____ **10.** Mr. DePalma

_____ **11.** Eugene's mother

_____ **12.** Roger

_____ **13.** Mrs. Luella Bates Washington Jones

_____ **14.** Kazuo

_____ **15.** Kazuo's mother

Column B

a. " . . . a large, big-boned woman with rough, man-working hands."

b. " . . . a short, stocky man. Hair is all over his head a foot long and hanging from his chin like a kinky mule tail."

c. " . . . fat and bald-headed . . . [with] an expression of winning gentleness and simplicity upon his tranquil countenance."

d. "He looked as if were fourteen or fifteen, frail and willow-wild, in tennis shoes and blue jeans.

e. "He was the curiousest man about always betting on anything that turned up."

f. " . . . my knuckles were turning red and raw from the jump rope . . . I hated my skinny flatchested body."

g. "She has been like this, chin on chest, eyes on ground, feet in shuffle, ever since the fire."

h. "She complained of pains in her neck. . . . Her doctor had previously diagnosed her symptoms as arthritis, but her death was sudden."

i. "She was a large woman with a large purse."

j. "[He had] a beautiful voice that rose and fell over words in a strange, lilting way. The kids at school called him 'the hick' and made fun of the way he talked."

k. "She had a halo of red hair floating over a delicate ivory face—the face of a doll—with freckles on the nose. Her smudged eye make-up made her look unreal . . . like a mannequin."

l. [He had] spindly legs . . . [and] was unable to walk."

m. "Earrings gold, too, and hanging down to her shoulders. Bracelets dangling and making noises when she moves her arm up to shake the folds of the dress out of her armpits."

n. "A short, muscular man with slicked-down black hair. . . . His voice broke, and he covered his face with his hands. His barrel chest was heaving."

o. " . . . has mossy teeth in an earnest face."

Unit 4 Review, continued

Part B Directions   Match each short story in Column C with three objects,
or props, from the story in Column D.

Column C

_____ **1.** "The Celebrated Jumping Frog of
Calaveras County"

_____ **2.** "Everyday Use"

_____ **3.** "American History"

_____ **4.** "Thank You, M'am"

_____ **5.** "Unfinished Message"

Column D

a. a jump rope, weeds, books

b. a barroom stove, quail shot, a horse

c. a purse, warm water, cocoa

d. a wheelchair, a window, a train

e. quilts, brightly colored dress, a churn top

About Suspense in the Short Story

Part A Directions On the line, write the letter of the answer that correctly completes each sentence.

1. Short stories of suspense are among the most _____ forms of literature.
   a. hated **b.** feared **c.** popular **d.** disliked

2. In this kind of _____, readers aren't certain what will happen next.
   a. poetry **b.** fiction **c.** nonfiction **b.** biography

3. With suspense stories, readers are often unable to predict the next happening in the _____.
   a. plot **b.** character **c.** symbol **d.** simile

4. In some stories, readers know much more than the _____ do.
   a. fables **b.** animals **c.** personifications **d.** characters

5. _____ for something to happen creates suspense for the reader.
   a. Writing **b.** Waiting **c.** Predicting **d.** Dictating

6. In other stories, the characters know more than the _____ know.
   a. animals **b.** personifications **c.** readers **d.** film directors

7. Authors _____ by placing clues in a story to hint at what will happen next.
   a. foreshadow **b.** personify **c.** lie **d.** narrate

Part B Directions Read each sentence. Write *T* if the statement is true or *F* if it is not true.

_____ **1.** Many people consider Alfred Hitchcock to be a master of suspense.

_____ **2.** This unit contains eight stories.

_____ **3.** Suspense writers take the expected and turn it into something new.

_____ **4.** Only readers in the United States enjoy stories of suspense.

_____ **5.** Many people enjoy a little hint of danger and the unexpected.

_____ **6.** Sometimes authors foreshadow events by using a certain setting.

_____ **7.** In all suspense stories, the readers know more than the characters.

_____ **8.** Sometimes suspense authors present a setting that seems normal.

The Lady, or the Tiger?

Part A Directions   Circle the word or term in parentheses that most accurately retells the story.

1. Long ago, there lived a (semibarbaric/democratic) king.

2. He had a beautiful (wife/daughter).

3. It was his custom to use a public (baseball stadium/arena) to decide the fate of people who were suspected of doing wrong.

4. In this place, the person had to choose a certain (door/wall).

5. Behind one was a vicious (tiger/lion); behind the other was a beautiful lady.

6. If the person chose the one with the vicious animal behind it, he would immediately be (killed/rescued).

7. If the person chose the one with the lady behind it, he would immediately be (killed/married).

8. The (boyfriend/brother) of the princess was to be the next victim.

9. To help him make his choice, the princess found out which door the (lady/tiger) stood behind.

10. When the challenge began, he looked to her for a clue, and she gestured to the door (on the right/on the left).

Workbook

The Lady, or the Tiger?, continued

Part B Directions   Note that facts are true statements. Opinions are statements that tell what a person prefers or thinks. Look at each sentence below and decide if it is a Fact or an Opinion. Write *Fact* or *Opinion* on the line in front of each sentence.

_____ **1.** The king was one of the main characters of this story.

_____ **2.** The most interesting character was the princess.

_____ **3.** The princess knew which door the lady stood behind.

_____ **4.** The young man trusted the princess to indicate the lady's door.

_____ **5.** This story was written by Frank Stockton.

_____ **6.** Stockton is the least famous of all the authors of suspense.

_____ **7.** Stockton is not very good at writing suspenseful stories.

_____ **8.** The king is the most evil character in this story.

_____ **9.** The lady waiting behind the door loved the man more than the princess did.

_____ **10.** After the climax, or high point of action, a suspenseful story will usually show how a problem is solved, but this story does something else.

The Lottery

Part A Directions   Write *True* if the statement is true; write *False* if the statement is not true. Write your answers on the lines provided before each statement. Make each false statement true by drawing a line through its underlined word. Then write the correct word below the statement.

_____ **1.** The author of "The Lottery" is <u>Shirley Jackson</u>.

     _____

_____ **2.** The story is about a small town that holds a lottery every <u>July</u> 27th.

     _____

_____ **3.** The first to assemble were the <u>adults</u>.

     _____

_____ **4.** They began to make a pile of <u>hay</u>.

     _____

_____ **5.** Mr. <u>Summers</u> conducted the lottery as he did most civic activities.

     _____

_____ **6.** The night before the lottery, he prepared the slips of paper and put them in a black <u>briefcase</u>.

     _____

_____ **7.** The first names he read were heads of <u>families</u>.

     _____

_____ **8.** Afterward, all the slips of <u>wood</u> were open.

     _____

_____ **9.** The <u>Hutchinson</u> family won the first part of the lottery.

     _____

_____ **10.** Tessie, Bill Hutchinson's <u>daughter</u>, won the final prize.

     _____

The Lottery, continued

Part B Directions   Match the sentence beginnings in Column A with the sentence endings in Column B. By doing this, create a true sentence about this short story. Write the letter of the correct answer on the line.

Column A

_____ 1. The people of the village began to gather . . .

_____ 2. The children assembled first and began to . . .

_____ 3. Mr. Summers put the black wooden box . . .

_____ 4. During the rest of the year, the townspeople kept the box . . .

_____ 5. The last person to arrive was Mrs. Hutchinson who . . .

_____ 6. Mrs. Dunbar drew the slip for her husband because . . .

_____ 7. At first the heads of families came up to Mr. Summers . . .

_____ 8. After that, they looked at their slips and discovered . . .

_____ 9. Mrs. Hutchinson shouted out that Mr. Summers . . .

_____ 10. When they drew again, Tessie Hutchinson . . .

Column B

a. . . . stuff their pockets full of stones.

b. . . . had not given her husband enough time to draw the paper he wanted.

c. . . . he had broken his leg before the lottery.

d. . . . in the square around ten o'clock.

e. . . . came hurriedly along the path to the square.

f. . . . which family was the one who would lose a member that year.

g. . . . in one place one year and in another place another year.

h. . . . and reached into the black box and took out a folded paper.

i. . . . had the slip with the black spot on it.

j. . . . on a three-legged stood in the center of the square.

The Fog Horn

Part A Directions   Unscramble the word groups below to make a true statement. On the line, write the four letters of the statement in their correct order.

1. **a.** hears the sound of the ocean
   b. before the story begins a man
   c. and decides to build a Fog Horn
   d. so everyone can hear the sound of eternity

   _____

2. **a.** November evening with the Fog Horn
   b. of the tower
   c. bumbling in the high throat
   d. the story begins on a cold

   _____

3. **a.** that something will happen
   b. each year for the last three years
   c. McDunn tells the narrator
   d. that night and that it has happened

   _____

4. **a.** McDunn believes that a monster
   b. subterranean depths of the ocean
   c. has waited alone for a million years in the
   d. to hear the voice of a friend

   _____

5. **a.** and then, from the surface of the sea,
   b. with a long, long neck
   c. the narrator suddenly sees a bit of froth,
   d. comes a large dark-colored head

   _____

6. **a.** and the monster answers,
   b. and when the Fog Horn blows again,
   c. the monster answers again
   d. the Fog Horn blows,

   _____

7. **a.** and then it rears up and
   b. after McDunn turns off the Fog Horn,
   c. the monster listens to the silence and rumbles,
   d. rushes at the tower

   _____

8. **a.** the monster destroys
   b. with its mournful cries
   c. the tower and then fills the night air
   d. but it hears no answer

   _____

The Fog Horn, continued

Part B Directions   Use the terms in the Word Bank
to complete each set of sentences below.

```
                        Word Bank
Bradbury          dinosaur          Illinois
narrator          California        fish
lighthouse        November          cards
fog horns         McDunn            roller coaster
```

1. The author of this suspenseful short story is Ray _____. He was born in the state of
   _____.

2. One day he was walking along a beach in _____. An old _____ there got
   him thinking.

3. One night, he heard the loud, sad sound of _____. This sound was all he needed to
   create his monster who was a _____, who is more than a million years old.

4. In the story, _____, the lighthouse master, talks about the strange things he has seen.
   One night he saw all the _____ in the sea surface beyond the lighthouse.

5. The _____ reports what the lighthouse master believes about the monster. This
   creature from the ocean floor has surfaced for the past three years in the month of
   _____.

6. To tell the story, the author uses many similes. For instance, he says that the Fog Horn in the
   _____ startles the gulls away like decks of scattered _____.

The Monkey's Paw

Directions Place each event in its correct order. Write the letter of the first event from "The Monkey's Paw" after #1. Write the letter of the second event from the story after #2 and so on. Note that #20 will be the last event.

Events in Order

#1. _____

#2. _____

#3. _____

#4. _____

#5. _____

#6. _____

#7. _____

#8. _____

#9. _____

#10. _____

List of Events to Be Put in Order

a. Sergeant-Major Morris sits downs and tells stories about India.

b. Morris begs White to pitch the paw in the fire again.

c. Herbert goes to work the next day.

d. Mr. White plays chess with his son, Herbert, while Mrs. White knits.

e. Mr. White wishes his son alive again.

f. The stranger tells the Whites that as compensation Herbert's firm will pay them two hundred pounds.

g. Morris tells the Whites that a fakir in India put a spell on the paw.

h. Morris leaves the Whites' home.

i. In the dark of the night, Mrs. White runs to the door.

j. They hear a knock at the door, and Mr. White goes to answer.

The Monkey's Paw, continued

#11. _____

#12. _____

#13. _____

#14. _____

#15. _____

#16. _____

#17. _____

#18. _____

#19. _____

#20. _____

k. A stranger comes and says he is from Herbert's place of business

l. Mr. White makes his third, and last, wish.

m. Morris throws the paw into the fire, and White rescues it.

n. After a long week passes, Mrs. White insists that Mr. White make a second wish.

o. Morris shows the Whites a mummified monkey's paw.

p. Mr. and Mrs. White, alone in the dark house, hear a faint knocking at the door.

q. Morris says that if White must keep the paw and make three wishes, he should at least wish for something sensible.

r. The stranger announces that Herbert is dead.

s. Morris explains that one man plus himself has had three wishes on the paw and that there are three wishes left for another man.

t. Mr. White wishes for two hundred pounds.

Red Moccasins

Part A Directions   Match each character's name in Column A with his or her description in Column B. Write the letter of each correct answer on the line.

Column A

_____ **1.** Chaske

_____ **2.** Clifford Blue Kettle

_____ **3.** Dina

_____ **4.** Emery

_____ **5.** Joyce

Column B

a. "[She was] long-legged and graceful, thick braids grazing her narrow hips. Her little heart-shaped face was dark brown, the color of a full-blood, and her eyes black as onyx studs."

b. "He was amiable and slow-minded. He longed to please."

c. "She giggled into a white handkerchief, tears rolling down her flat cheeks. Her short hair was patchy, singed in several places."

d. "[He] was sturdy and tall for his age, his powerful calf muscles bulging like little crab apples under the skin. His hair was creamy yellow, the color of beeswax, and his eyes were a silvery gray, so pale they were almost white."

e. "He was such a giant he seemed uncomfortable in his body; his posture, an accommodating stoop, and his gestures, apologetic. Off the ice he shambled awkwardly."

Red Moccasins, continued

Part B Directions   Complete the crossword puzzle by using the fifteen words in the Word Bank.

Across

2. The narrator made her niece a pair of _____.
5. At the end of the story, red _____ are scattered outside the narrator's home.
6. The narrator called on her _____ before the death of her niece.
7. The narrator filled her dead husband's pockets with _____ drop candies before he was buried.
10. As the story began, the narrator's son was beating on a pillow and making a _____ song.
11. After her son's death, the narrator threw her _____ at her cousin Joyce.
12. The narrator put two pairs of ice _____ in her husband's coffin.
13. Because it was winter, the bodies of the narrator's son and her niece rested in the _____ for two months.

Down

1. The name of the wild horse that killed the narrator's husband, Emery, was _____.
2. The name of Chaske's pet owlet was _____.
3. The disease that killed Chaske was _____.
4. The name of the narrator's son was _____.
5. The name of the narrator's niece was _____.
8. Max was an _____.
9. The color of the beads on the niece's moccasins was _____.

Word Bank
beads
consumption
icehouse
Max
owlet
Bernardine
dresses
lemon
moccasins
powwow
Chaske
grandmother
Lutheran
red
skates

Unit 5 Review

Part A Directions   Match each cause in Column A with its result, or effect in Column B. Write the letter of each correct answer on the line. Remember that a cause is something that makes a result, or an effect, happen. Note that each of the five stories in the unit is listed in the order that the stories were presented.

Column A

_____ 1. The king wanted to punish crime and reward virtue impartially.

_____ 2. An accused person would open one of the doors.

_____ 3. The princess knew the door behind which the lady stood.

_____ 4. Mr. Summers said, "All ready?"

_____ 5. The heads of the families opened their slips of paper.

_____ 6. Mrs. Hutchinson had the slip with the black spot on it.

_____ 7. The Fog Horn blew.

_____ 8. McDunn turned off the Fog Horn.

_____ 9. The monster killed what it loved most in the world.

_____ 10. Sergeant-Major Morris told the Whites that three wishes were left on the monkey's paw.

_____ 11. Mr. White wished for two thousand pounds.

_____ 12. Mr. White wished his son would come back from the dead.

_____ 13. Many people in North Dakota were dying of consumption, or tuberculosis.

_____ 14. The narrator did magic and summoned her niece from her house.

_____ 15. The narrator's magic took on a life of its own.

Column B

a. So the townspeople stoned her to death.

b. He would then be eaten alive by a tiger or married to a beautiful lady.

c. So his son, Herbert, died.

d. So it settled back in the deepest Deeps to wait another million years.

e. Then Bill Hutchinson discovered he had the winning lottery ticket.

f. So she continued to hear the stamp of shuffle of her niece's steps as she danced outside, around the narrator's clapboard house.

g. So he built an arena with two doors.

h. And the monster answered.

i. So a knocking came at the door and White made his third, and last, wish.

j. So the narrator's son, Chaske, got ill and died.

k. So the people gathered in the square became quiet, wetting their lips, not looking around.

l. So Dina danced in the cold until she died.

m. So the monster destroyed the lighthouse.

n. So the Whites wanted to obtain the paw.

o. So she gestured to the right.

Unit 5 Review, continued

Part B Directions   Match each story in Column C with one of its settings in Column D. Write the letter of each correct answer on the line.

Column C

_____ **1.** "The Lady, or the Tiger?"

_____ **2.** "The Lottery"

_____ **3.** "The Fog Horn"

_____ **4.** "The Monkey's Paw"

_____ **5.** "Red Moccasins"

Column D

a. " . . . a shallow frozen pond. The ice was uneven, marred by tangled clumps of weeds."

b. "The vast amphitheatre, with its encircling galleries, its mysterious vaults, and its unseen passages, was an agent of poetic justice."

c. "Without, the night was cold and wet; but in the small parlor of Laburnam Villa the blinds were drawn and the fire burned brightly."

d. "There wasn't a town for a hundred miles down the coast, just a road which came lonely through dead country to the sea, with few cars on it, a stretch of two miles of cold water out to our rock, and rare few ships."

e. "The morning of June 27th was clear and sunny, with the fresh warmth of a full-summer day; the flowers were blossoming profusely and the grass was richly green."

About Nonfiction

Directions   Circle the word or term in parentheses that accurately completes the statement.

1. Nonfiction is factual (prose/poetic) writing.

2. Biographies, autobiographies, and (novels/essays) are nonfiction.

3. In general, prose writing that is not fiction is (poetry/nonfiction).

4. Nonfiction concerns (real/made-up) people and facts.

5. Readers expect nonfiction to present (facts/made-up characters).

6. Readers expect nonfiction to deal with (fictional/real) events.

7. Nonfiction has a specific (setting/purpose), such as to describe or explain.

8. The form of nonfiction known as (biography/autobiography) is written by someone other than the person whose life is being described.

9. The form of nonfiction known as (biography/autobiography) is written by the person about himself or herself.

10. The (American/French) writer Michel de Montaigne developed the essay.

11. The French term *J'essai*, from which we get the word *essay*, means ("I lie."/"I try.")

12. Like short stories, essays are (brief/very long).

13. A nonfiction narrative tells a true story, usually in (chronological order/flashback).

14. Personal accounts may be in the form of a (novel/diary).

15. Nonfiction is a very (narrow/broad) category of literature.

Kon-Tiki

Part A Directions   Use the words in the Word Bank to complete each sentence below.

Word Bank		
balsa	elephants	Norway
Polynesia	whales	bamboo
fathoms	Peru	sun
zoology		

1. Thor Heyerdahl, the author of *Kon-Tiki*, was born in _____.

2. As a youth, he studied _____, the science of animals.

3. In 1947, he and five others built a _____ -wood raft to prove a theory.

4. They built a _____ cabin on the raft.

5. They called their raft the *Kon-Tiki* after the Peruvian _____ god.

6. They sailed from the country of _____ in South America.

7. They wanted to prove that the first settlers in _____ could have come from South America.

8. They met real monsters whose visible parts were five _____, or thirty feet, long.

9. The ocean creatures were bigger than land-based _____.

10. They were not marine-based _____ because they never came up to breathe.

Kon-Tiki, continued

Part B Directions   Match each cause in Column A with its result, or effect in Column B. Write the letter of each correct answer on the line. Remember that a cause is something that makes a result, or an effect, happen.

Column A

_____ **1.** As night fell, single glowing plankton flashed around the raft.

_____ **2.** Sometimes two round shining eyes suddenly rose and glared at the crew with an unblinking hypnotic stare.

_____ **3.** The crew threw overboard the guts of two dolphins.

_____ **4.** A twenty-five-pound dolphin was hanging behind the raft.

_____ **5.** The whale shark appeared inert and stupid.

_____ **6.** The whale shark circled the raft for barely an hour.

_____ **7.** The crew members encouraged Erik to harpoon the whale shark.

_____ **8.** A second or two passed before the whale shark realized what had happened.

_____ **9.** The whale shark stood on its head and plunged down into the ocean depths.

_____ **10.** The whale shark seemed extremely angry.

Column B

a. So they were sometimes scared because they did not know what was staring at them.

b. But the crew felt that it had been there for much longer.

c. So the whale shark swam toward it.

d. Then he turned into a mountain of steel muscles.

e. So the crew drew in their bare legs when the glowing pellets washed around them.

f. Then the crew saw a cascade of water as the giant disappeared.

g. So the crew shouted with laughter.

h. So he thrust the harpoon into the shark's gristly head.

i. So the crew waited in fear for him to appear again.

j. So a whale shark came up to eat.

A Celebration of Grandfathers

Part A Directions Unscramble the word groups below to make a true statement. On the line, write the four letters of the statement in their correct order.

1. **a.** the phrase "Buenos días le de Dios, abuelo,"   _____
    b. the author was taught to
    c. which means "God give you a good day, grandfather"
    d. greet his grandfather with

2. **a.** who gave him a wise path   _____
    b. of life to follow
    c. were strong in their beliefs and
    d. the author remembers old people who

3. **a.** these old people   _____
    b. were from the cultures of the Rio Grande,
    c. whom he remembers
    d. and they lived side by side with one another

4. **a.** and cycles of time and they knew   _____
    b. how to prepare the earth
    c. they knew the rhythms
    d. in the spring for planting

5. **a.** but they have just come in contact   _____
    b. newcomers to New Mexico often say
    c. with the inner strength of the people
    d. that time seems to move slowly,

6. **a.** and walrus-mustached and he stood   _____
    b. he was a giant
    c. five feet tall, but to the child
    d. the author's grandfather was bearded

7. **a.** in the valley called Puerto de Luna where   _____
    b. in his childhood summers, the author
    c. went to live
    d. his grandfather farmed

8. **a.** and the young plants died, the   _____
    b. author's grandfather simply said,
    c. when the summer was dry
    d. "Pray for rain"

A Celebration of Grandfathers, continued

9. **a.** next to his grandfather   _____
   b. sometimes the author
   c. who smelled of orchards and fields
   d. got to ride in a wagon

10. **a.** even when he was old and sick   _____
    b. the grandfather continued to smoke
    c. because he said that he liked
    d. to see the smoke rise

Part B Directions   Read each sentence. Write _T_ if the statement is true
or _F_ if it is not true.

_____ **1.** Rudolfo Anaya has been called the father of modern Mexican-American literature.

_____ **2.** He was born in Canada in 1937.

_____ **3.** "A Celebration of Grandfathers" is a short story that is not true.

_____ **4.** The author says that we have all felt time stand still.

_____ **5.** One of the things his grandfather told him was "Know where you stand."

_____ **6.** When a young woman was dragged by a horse and died, his grandfather said,
"Death is only this small transformation in life."

_____ **7.** The author grew up speaking French.

_____ **8.** Learning English was difficult for him.

_____ **9.** His grandfather told him not to learn English.

_____ **10.** When things were hard for the author, his grandfather would say, "Ten paciencia,"
which means "Have patience."

Of Dry Goods and Black Bow Ties

Part A Directions   Note that facts are true statements. Opinions are statements that tell what a person prefers or thinks. Look at each sentence below and decide if it is a Fact or an Opinion. Write *Fact* or *Opinion* on the line in front of each sentence.

_____ **1.** "Of Dry Good and Black Bow Ties" is the best piece of nonfiction every written about the Japanese people in America.

_____ **2.** Its author is Yoshiko Uchida.

_____ **3.** She studied at the University of California in Berkeley.

_____ **4.** In her biographical essay, we meet Shozo Shimada.

_____ **5.** Mr. Shimada is the saddest character in any biographical essay.

_____ **6.** Mr. Shimada was not a success as a human being because he lost all his money.

_____ **7.** The proof that the author's father was a success is that he wrote a letter to Mr. Shimada.

_____ **8.** When Mr. Shimada came to the author's home he was selling *The Book of Knowledge*.

_____ **9.** Mr. Shimada said that it took him ten years to pay back every cent he owed.

_____ **10.** The black bow tie in the story is one of the best symbols ever used in a piece of nonfiction.

Of Dry Goods and Black Bow Ties, continued

Part B Directions   Match the sentence beginnings in Column A with the sentence endings in Column B. By doing this, create true sentences about this biographical essay. Write the letter of the correct answer on the line.

Column A

_____ **1.** During World War II, Yoshiko Uchida and her family . . .

_____ **2.** In her biographical essay, we meet her father . . .

_____ **3.** Mr. Shimada was Seattle's most . . .

_____ **4.** He had come to American in 1880 and realized quickly . . .

_____ **5.** He bought a second-hand sewing machine . . .

_____ **6.** Soon he began the first . . .

_____ **7.** Mr. Shimada hired the author's father . . .

_____ **8.** The author's father worked with Mr. Shimada for ten years, . . .

_____ **9.** In the Great Depression of 1929, . . .

_____ **10.** Toward the end of the biographical essay, . . .

Column B

a. . . . successful Japanese business man.

b. . . . becoming first the buyer for his Seattle store and later, manager of the Portland branch.

c. . . . and hung a dressmaker's sign in his window.

d. . . . and his first employer, Mr. Shozo Shimada.

e. . . . Mr. Shimada returns, penniless, to Japan.

f. . . . that he could not compete with American laborers whose bodies were twice his in muscle and bulk.

g. . . . because he was quick to sense his need for a job.

h. . . . were forced to move to an internment camp in the Southwest desert.

i. . . . Mr. Shimada's banks failed.

j. . . . Shimada Dry Goods Store on State Street.

Gather Together in My Name

Directions On the line, write the letter of the answer that correctly completes each sentence.

1. Maya Angelou was born in _____ , Missouri, in 1928.

   a. Kansas City   **b.** Hannibal
   c. Stamps   **d.** St. Louis

2. Angelou read one of her poems at the inauguration of President _____.

   a. Reagan   **b.** Bush
   c. Clinton   **d.** Roosevelt

3. The excerpt is from one of her _____ books.

   a. biographical   **b.** autobiographical
   c. fiction   **d.** poetry

4. She tells us that R. L. Poole had heard about her at the _____.

   a. restaurant   **b.** movie theater
   c. record shop   **d.** post office

5. Poole asked her if she was a _____

   a. writer   **b.** poet
   c. dancer   **d.** trapeze artist

6. Poole had come from _____.

   a. Kansas City   **b.** St. Louis
   c. New York   **d.** Chicago

7. Poole was looking for a _____ for his act.

   a. partner   **b.** dog
   c. cat   **d.** snake

8. Angelou told Poole that she could do the _____.

   a. split   **b.** tap-dance
   c. acrobatics   **d.** jazz

9. In the next few minutes, Poole witnessed his strangest _____.

   a. meal   **b.** audition
   c. television show   **d.** soap opera

10. At the end of the excerpt, Poole tells Angelou that she has nice _____.

    a. eyes   **b.** feet
    c. legs   **d.** hair

The Story of My Life

Directions   Complete the crossword puzzle by using the fifteen words in the Word Bank.

Across

2. The genius of the author's _____ made life beautiful.
4. The author learned something about life from a _____ that jumped out of its glass globe.
7. A child's mind is like a _____.
9. At the beginning of her work with her teacher, the author was full of _____.
10. _____ was the author's one hard school subject.
13. She and her teacher did much learning in the _____.
14. Anne _____ was the author's teacher.

Down

1. _____ person cannot hear.
3. The author attended _____ College.
5. The author's teacher learned how to teach the blind in _____.
6. The author and her teacher walked to the _____ River.
8. The author's name is Helen _____.
9. The author's teacher studied at the _____ Institution for the Blind.
11. With the help of a good teacher, a child's mind becomes a mighty _____.
12. A _____ person cannot see.

Word Bank
arithmetic
brook
Perkins
teacher
river
blind
possibilities
Sullivan
Tennessee
deaf
Boston
Keller
Radcliffe
tadpole
woods

Into Thin Air

Part A Directions   Write *True* if the statement is true; write *False* if the statement is not true. Write your answers on the lines provided before each statement. Make each false statement true by drawing a line through its underlined word. Then write the correct word below the statement.

_____   **1.**   The author of *Into Thin Air* is <u>Jon Krakauer</u>.

         _____

_____   **2.**   Some people who wanted to climb Mount <u>McKinley</u> paid as much as $65,000.

         _____

_____   **3.**   One danger in climbing is *hypoxia,* or lack of <u>hydrogen</u>.

         _____

_____   **4.**   A senior <u>student</u> leads the way up Hillary Step.

         _____

_____   **5.**   It is one of the most famous pitches in all of mountaineering, being <u>forty</u> feet of rock and ice.

         _____

_____   **6.**   The author reaches the summit of the mountain on <u>December</u> 10, 1996.

         _____

_____   **7.**   At the summit of the mountain, the author feels dread because he now has to <u>ascend</u> the mountain.

         _____

_____   **8.**   The storm becomes a <u>blizzard</u> with winds gusting in excess of 60 knots.

         _____

_____   **9.**   He is headed toward Camp <u>Three</u>

         _____

_____   **10.**   Later, he learns that the storm has stranded <u>nineteen</u> men and women on the mountain.

         _____

Into Thin Air, continued

Part B Directions Place each event in its correct order. Write the letter of the first event from the excerpt *Into Thin Air* after #1. Write the letter of the second event from the story after #2 and so on. Note that #10 will be the last event.

Events in Order

#1. _____

#2. _____

#3. _____

#4. _____

#5. _____

#6. _____

#7. _____

#8. _____

#9. _____

#10. _____

List of Events to Be Put in Order

a. Boukreev, a senior guide, leads the author and others up the pitch.

b. Rising to his feet, Krakauer now sees Andy Harris, whose face is coated with frost.

c. Krakauer continues through the blizzard as his oxygen runs out.

d. By 6:30 P.M., Krakauer has descended to within 200 vertical feet of Camp Four; he can see the tents, but he is so tired that he sits down.

e. Krakauer feels dread as he realizes that now he must descend the mountain.

f. With no supplemental oxygen, Krakauer begins to move more slowly.

g. Krakauer reaches the summit of Mount Everest.

h. Krakauer does crampon work, comes safely to the bottom of an incline, walks into Camp Four, and reaches his tent, safely.

i. Krakauer hears the sound of thunder and faces a blizzard with gusting winds.

j. Krakauer comes to the foot of Hillary Step, a forty-foot, near-vertical pitch of rock and ice.

Unit 6 Review

Part A Directions   Match each author's name in Column A with the correct title in Column B. Write the letter of each correct answer on the line.

Column A	Column B
_____ **1.** Thor Heyerdahl	**a.** *The Story of My Life*
_____ **2.** Rudolfo A. Anaya	**b.** "Of Dry Goods and Black Bow Ties"
_____ **3.** Yoshiko Uchida	**c.** *Kon-Tiki*
_____ **4.** Maya Angelou	**d.** *Into Thin Air*
_____ **5.** Helen Keller	**e.** *Gather Together in My Name*
_____ **6.** Jon Krakauer	**f.** "A Celebration of Grandfathers"

Unit 6 Review, continued

Part B Directions   Use the words in the Word Bank to complete each set of sentences below.

> **Word Bank**
>
> autobiography   essay   humor
> old   Shimada   book
> Everest   Japanese   personal
> Sullivan   dignity   excerpt
> Mexican   raft

1. The excerpt from the _____ Kon-Tiki describes a strange encounter with a real-life sea monster. The crew made a 4,000 mile trip across the Pacific by _____.

2. In the reflective _____ "A Celebration of Grandfathers," the author honors his grandfather. He also honors _____ -American traditions and all _____ people.

3. The biographical essay "Of Dry Goods and Black Bow Ties" gives readers a glimpse into the life of _____ immigrants. It also tells about Mr. _____ who did not lose his _____ , despite losing his wealth.

4. In the _____ from the autobiography *Gather Together in My Name*, the author looks back with _____ at an embarrassing moment.

5. In the excerpt from the _____ *The Story of My Life*, the author describes how her teacher helped her learn about life. Anne _____ gave new life to this deaf and blind author.

6. *Into Thin Air* is the author's _____ account of an expedition up Mount _____. The expedition proved deadly for some of the climbers.

About Poetry

Directions   On the line, write the letter of the answer that correctly completes each sentence.

1. Poetry is a _____ form of literature.

   a. long   **b.** short   **c.** suspense   **d.** short story

2. Some of the poems in this unit are _____, or songs.

   a. novels   **b.** suspense fiction   **c.** ballads   **d.** prose

3. Poetry is literature in _____ form.

   a. nonfiction   **b.** fiction   **c.** novel   **d.** verse

4. Verse means that poems have particular kinds of _____.

   a. characters   **b.** images   **c.** settings   **d.** rhythm

5. Poems are often divided into groups of lines called _____.

   a. paragraphs   **b.** sentences   **c.** stanzas   **d.** periods

6. Each word the poet uses has _____ and meaning.

   a. sound   **b.** sight   **c.** taste   **d.** touch

7. Poets use _____, which is the repetition of beginning sounds.

   a. onomatopoeia   **b.** alliteration   **c.** symbol   **d.** images

8. Poets also use _____, which is the use of words that sound like their meaning.

   a. onomatopoeia   **b.** alliteration   **c.** symbol   **d.** images

9. Poets use _____ instead of sentences and stanzas instead of paragraphs.

   a. periods   **b.** questions   **c.** lines   **d.** the alphabet

10. Rhyming words are words that end in the same _____.

    a. sound   **b.** letter   **c.** vowel   **d.** consonant

A Red, Red Rose

Directions   Use the words in the Word Bank to complete each sentence below.

> **Word Bank**
>
> | century | hyperbole | New Year's Eve | rhyme | song |
> |---------|-----------|----------------|-------|------|
> | dialect | melodie | pretty | simile | thousand |

1. "A Red, Red Rose" was first published as a _____.

2. It was written by Robert Burns in the eighteenth _____.

3. It is written in Burns's native Scots _____.

4. The lines "And I will luve thee still, my dear,/Till a' the seas gang dry" is an example of _____, or poetic exaggeration.

5. "O, my luve's like a red, red rose" is an example of a _____.

6. A "bonnie lass" is a _____ girl.

7. In the poem, Burns says he will come back to his love even if he has gone ten _____ miles away.

8. The poet says his love is like a red rose and like a _____.

9. The _____ scheme of this poem is a/b/c/b.

10. Burns also wrote "Auld Lang Syne," which many people sing on _____.

The Streets of Laredo

Directions   Write *True* if the statement is true; write *False* is the statement is not true. Write your answers on the lines provided before each statement. Make each false statement true by drawing a line through its underlined word and writing the correct word or words below the statement.

_____   **1.** "The Streets of Laredo" is a traditional <u>European</u> ballad.

    _____

_____   **2.** The cowboy in the ballad died in Laredo, <u>New York</u>.

    _____

_____   **3.** Traditional folk ballads tell simple stories and probably were <u>sung</u> as well as spoken.

    _____

_____   **4.** The <u>young</u> cowboy in the ballad is also a gambler.

    _____

_____   **5.** There is a change of speakers between the first and the second <u>paragraphs</u> of the ballad.

    _____

_____   **6.** The cowboy says that he has done <u>wrong</u>.

    _____

_____   **7.** He asks the town to get six "jolly <u>salesmen</u>" to carry his coffin.

    _____

_____   **8.** He asks the town to bury his <u>spear</u> and his six-shooter with him.

    _____

_____   **9.** The dead cowboy was wrapped up in <u>black</u> linen

    _____

_____   **10.** He asks the town to beat the drums <u>slowly</u> for him.

    _____

Ballad of Birmingham

Part A Directions   Place each event in its correct order. Write the letter of the first event from "Ballad of Birmingham" after #1. Write the letter of the second event from the ballad after #2 and so on. Note that #5 will be the last event.

Events in Order   **List of Events to Be Put in Order**

#1. _____   **a.** The young girl puts white shoes on her feet and goes to church.

#2. _____   **b.** A young girl asks to march the streets of Birmingham in a Freedom March.

#3. _____   **c.** The mother hears an explosion and races through the streets.

#4. _____   **d.** The young girl's mother says no because marching will be dangerous.

#5. _____   **e.** The mother smiles because she knows her child is in a sacred place.

Part B Directions   Read each sentence. Write *T* if the statement is true or *F* if it is not true.

_____ **1.** The city of Birmingham, where the bombing took place, is in Alabama.

_____ **2.** The mother does not let her young daughter go to the Freedom March.

_____ **3.** The young daughter disobeys her mother and goes to the march.

_____ **4.** The mother races through the streets of Birmingham, calling for the firemen to come.

_____ **5.** At the end of the poem, the mother is dead.

Blesséd Lord, what it is to be young *and* WE REAL COOL

Directions Each sentence has one missing word, term, number, or proper name. Below each are three words, terms, numbers, or proper names. One of these completes the sentence. Circle the letter of the one word, term, number, or proper name that completes the sentence.

1. David McCord published _____ poems.

   a. 127   **b.** 550   **c.** 1011

2. Most of his poems were written for _____ readers.

   a. young   **b.** old   **c.** women

3. A limerick is a five-line poem that is usually meant to _____.

   a. amuse   **b.** persuade   **c.** inform

4. In a limerick, the first, _____, and fifth lines end with words that rhyme.

   a. second   **b.** third   **c.** fourth

5. The words *enchanted* and *enthralled* and *caller* and *called* are examples of _____, or the use of words whose beginning sounds are the same.

   a. simile   **b.** metaphor   **c.** alliteration

6. Gwendolyn Brooks grew up in _____.

   a. Los Angeles   **b.** Chicago   **c.** New York

7. In her poem "WE REAL COOL," she captures the rhythms of her city's _____ halls.

   a. school   **b.** movie   **c.** pool

8. The jazzy style of "WE REAL COOL" gives the _____ shocking sentence a powerful effect.

   a. first   **b.** middle   **c.** final

9. Most of Gwendolyn Brooks's poetry is about _____-American life.

   a. Japanese   **b.** Native   **c.** African

10. The words *sin* and *gin* are examples of two words that _____.

   a. rhyme   **b.** couplet   **c.** simile

Jabberwocky

Directions Circle the word or words in parentheses that best complete each sentence.

1. The pen name of Charles Lutwidge Dodgson was Lewis (Brooks/Carroll).

2. He wrote during the (eighteenth/nineteenth) century.

3. He lived in (Great Britain/the United States).

4. He was both a writer and a (computer inventor/mathematician).

5. He was famous for playing with language and inventing (words/computer programs).

6. He invented *brillig,* which is the time for broiling (dinner/potatoes).

7. The words *snicker-snack* in stanza five of "Jabberwocky" are an example of (simile/alliteration) or the use of words whose beginning sounds are the same.

8. In the poem, a father tells his son to beware the (Lion/Jabberwock).

9. The father also tells him to beware the (Jubjub bird/Vulture).

10. The boy uses his (sword/gun) to kill the monster.

The Bells

Directions Complete the crossword puzzle by using the fifteen words in the Word Bank.

Across

1. "While the stars that _____ /All the heavens, seem to twinkle"
3. "To the swinging and the _____ /Of the bells, bells, bells—"
4. "And the people—ah, the people—/They that dwell up in the _____,"
5. "What a world of _____ their melody foretells!"
9. "To the turtle-dove that listens, while she gloats/On the _____!"
10. "What a tale of _____, now their turbulency tells!"
12. "Through the balmy air of night/How they ring out their _____—"

Down

2. "In the _____ of the night,/How we shiver with affright"
3. "Keeping time, time, time,/In a sort of Runic _____,"
4. "Too much horrified to speak,/They can only shriek, _____,"
5. "Hear the _____ wedding bells—/Golden bells!"
6. "To the _____ and the chiming of the bells!"
7. "How they tinkle, tinkle, _____, /In the icy air of night!"
8. "How the _____ ebbs and flows; Yet the ear distinctly tells,"
11. "For every sound that floats/From the _____ within their throats"

Word Bank

danger	ringing
delight	rust
mellow	shriek
merriment	silence
moon	steeple
oversprinkle	terror
rhyme	tinkle
rhyming	

Oranges

Part A Directions   Match the two lines of the poem in Column A with the line or lines in Column B that follow it. Write the letter of the correct answer on the line.

Column A

_____ **1.** "The first time I walked/With a girl, I was twelve,"/

_____ **2.** "Down a narrow aisle of goods./I turned to the candies"/

_____ **3.** "I took the nickel from/My pocket, then an orange,"/

_____ **4.** "Outside,/A few cars hissing past,"/

_____ **5.** "I took my girl's hand/In mine for two blocks,"/

Column B

a. "And set them quietly on/The counter."

b. "Tiered like bleachers,/And asked what she wanted—"

c. "Then released it to let/Her unwrap the chocolate."

d. "Fog hanging like old/Coats between the trees."

e. "Cold, and weighted down/With two oranges in my jacket."

Part B Directions   Read each sentence. Write *T* if the statement is true or *F* if it is not true.

_____ **1.** Gary Soto, who wrote "Oranges" is both a poet and a teacher.

_____ **2.** He draws many of his images from his Chinese heritage.

_____ **3.** The images in his poem help us see, hear, touch, smell, and taste his memory of walking with a girl for the first time.

_____ **4.** The rhyme scheme for this poem is a b a b.

_____ **5.** The poet uses several colors in his poem.

Be Like the Bird, Dreams, flock, *and* The Red Wheelbarrow

Directions Note that facts are true statements. Opinions are statements that tell what a person prefers or thinks. Look at each sentence below and decide if it is a Fact or an Opinion. Write *Fact* or *Opinion* on the line in front of each sentence.

_____ **1.** The best poem among these four is "The Red Wheelbarrow."

_____ **2.** Langston Hughes wrote the poem "Dreams."

_____ **3.** The poem with the most memorable image is "The Red Wheelbarrow" by William Carlos Williams.

_____ **4.** The rhyme scheme for "Dreams" is a b c b.

_____ **5.** "Be Like the Bird" is a silly poem.

_____ **6.** "flock" says that "snow moves like an ancient herd."

_____ **7.** The easiest poem to understand among these four is "Be Like the Bird."

_____ **8.** Few people who read "Dreams" will ever remember it.

_____ **9.** Langston Hughes asks the reader to "Hold fast to dreams."

_____ **10.** Short poems are always easier to understand than long poems.

The rooster's crowing *and* Haiku

Directions Use the words in the Word Bank to complete each set of lines below.

Word Bank				
convicts	gems	jazz	pencil	steel
flies	guards	knife	songs	teacup

1. "Eastern guard tower/glints in sunset; _____ rest/like lizards on rocks."

2. "The piano man/is sitting at 3 am/his _____ drop like plum."

3. "Morning sun slants cell./Drunks stagger like cripple _____/ On the Jailhouse floor."

4. "To write a blues song/Is to regiment riots/and pluck _____ from graves."

5. "A bare pecan tree/slips a _____ shadow down/a moonlit snow slope."

6. "The falling snow flakes/Can not blunt the hard aches nor/Match the _____ stillness."

7. "Under moon shadows/A tall boy flashes _____ and/Slices star bright ice."

8. "In the August grass/Struck by the last rays of sun/The cracked _____ screams."

9. "Making _____ swing in/Seventeen syllables AIN'T/No square poet's job."

10. "But at Osaka's gateway/The _____ are never fooled."

The Poet

Directions On the line, write the letter of the answer that correctly completes each sentence.

1. The author of the poem "The Poet" is _____.

    a. Robert Frost **b.** Edgar Allan Poe **c.** Gwendolyn Brooks **d.** Jane Hirshfield

2. The poem explores the quiet, rather _____ world of poets.

    a. exciting **b.** lonely **c.** January **d.** summer

3. The poem is especially about _____ poets, whose life and work remain unknown to the wider world.

    a. women **b.** men **c.** Chinese **d.** Japanese

4. The poem was first published in *The Atlantic Monthly* in _____.

    a. 1678 **b.** 1703 **c.** 1879 **d.** 1997

5. "The light of the lamp" is an example of _____.

    a. simile **b.** metaphor **c.** alliteration **d.** rhyme

6. The poem says that the poet's table is covered with _____.

    a. a tablecloth **b.** oranges **c.** feathers **d.** paper

7. The poet has taken the _____ off of the lamp.

    a. shade **b.** chain **c.** bottom **d.** bulb

8. Besides the lamp and the table, the poet also has a _____ in her room.

    a. bed **b.** chair **c.** cat **d.** footstool

9. The poet says "Let one or two she _____ be in the next room."

    a. nurtures **b.** feeds **c.** supports **d.** loves

10. The poet ends the poem by saying "Let her have _____, and silence, enough paper to make mistakes and go on."

    a. children **b.** sunlight **c.** time **d.** a husband

The Road Not Taken

Directions Write *True* if the statement is true; write *False* is the statement is not true. Write your answers on the lines provided before each statement. Make each false statement true by drawing a line through its underlined word and writing the correct word or words below the statement.

_____ **1.** Robert Frost is one of the <u>sixteenth</u> century's most important and honored poets.

_____

_____ **2.** "The Road Not Taken" is one of his <u>least</u>-known poems.

_____

_____ **3.** In his poem, Frost explains how a decision between which of two roads to take in a <u>desert</u> changed his life.

_____

_____ **4.** The rhyme scheme of each <u>stanza</u> is a b a a b.

_____

_____ **5.** The road he took was <u>grassy</u>.

_____

_____ **6.** Frost uses <u>end</u> rhyme in his poem.

_____

_____ **7.** He <u>sat</u> for a long time considering which road to take.

_____

_____ **8.** Both of the roads had <u>leaves</u> on them.

_____

_____ **9.** Frost says that he kept one road for another <u>day</u>.

_____

_____ **10.** Frost says that he "took the one <u>less</u> traveled by,/And that has made all the difference."

_____

In a Farmhouse *and* this morning (for the girls of eastern high school)

Directions Circle the word or term in parentheses that best completes each sentence.

1. Luis Omar Salinas's main subject is the experience of (Hispanic/Japanese) people in the United States

2. His poem "In a Farmhouse" is about a little boy who has worked all day in the (wheat/cotton) fields for $2.30.

3. The little boy is (eight/twelve) years old.

4. He wonders if the rest of the (Native Americans/Mestizos) are hungry that day.

5. He thinks that dying from (violence/hunger) is "an odd way to leave for heaven."

6. One of Lucille Clifton's main subjects for poetry is (Hispanic/African)-American girls and women.

7. In her poem "this morning," she skillfully uses (hyperbole/repetition)

8. She says that "this morning," she met (a friend/herself) "coming in."

9. The words "shining/quick as a snake/a tall/tree girl a" provides two examples of (alliteration/onomatopoeia).

10. "Quick as a snake" is an example of a (metaphor/simile) because it uses *as* to make a comparison.

My Life Story

Directions Note that facts are true statements. Opinions are statements that tell what a person prefers or thinks. Look at each sentence below and decide if it is a Fact or an Opinion. Write *Fact* or *Opinion* on the line in front of each sentence.

_____ 1. The poet who wrote "My Life Story" has suffered more than any other poet in this unit.

_____ 2. Using a metaphor, the poet compares herself to "a sand in the big desert"—one of millions with no power.

_____ 3. "My Life Story" has no definite rhyme scheme.

_____ 4. The attitude this poet takes toward her poem is more serious than Frost's attitude toward "The Road Not Taken."

_____ 5. Lan Nguyen is more gifted than the other poets in this unit.

_____ 6. The poet asks two questions in this poem.

_____ 7. The poem ends with the line "God cannot be mean to her forever."

_____ 8. This is best poem written about the Vietnam War.

_____ 9. Anyone who lives through a war can write a better poem than someone who has not lived through a war.

_____ 10. In her poem, the poet tells us that her "dearest father passed away/and left a big scar in the child's head."

A Headstrong Boy

Directions Complete the crossword puzzle by using the fifteen words in the Word Bank.

Across

1. "I want . . . to cover the world with colored _____."
2. "I'd like to draw . . . carefree, _____ rivers"
4. "I think I'll tear the paper to bits/and let them drift away,/hunting for _____."
5. "I'm a _____ boy."
7. "I'd like to _____"
9. "I want every instant/to be lovely as _____."
10. "I'd like to draw . . . a clumsy _____,"
11. "I'd like to draw _____,"

Down

1. "I'd like to draw . . . eyes that never _____,"
3. "I'd like to draw . . . an _____ love"
4. "I haven't any crayons,/any _____ moments."
5. "I'd like to draw . . . a bright _____,"
6. "I'd like to draw . . . an _____."
8. "Finally, I'd like to draw myself in one corner—/a _____"
10. "I'd like to draw . . . hills sheathed in green _____."

Word Bank

apple	crayons	freedom	horizon	rippling
breathless	dawn	furze	imaginary	wept
butterflies	draw	headstrong	panda	windows

Nikki-Rosa

Part A Directions   Match the line of the poem in Column A with the line in Column B that follows it. Write the letter of the correct answer on the line.

Column A

_____ **1.** "childhood remembrances are always a drag"/

_____ **2.** "they never talk about how happy you were to have your mother"/

_____ **3.** "your biographers never understand"/

_____ **4.** "it isn't your father's drinking that makes any difference"/

_____ **5.** "and I really hope no white person ever has cause to write about me"/

Column B

a. "all to yourself . . . "

b. "because they never understand Black love is Black wealth . . . "

c. "your father's pain as he sells his stock"

d. "but only that everybody is together . . . "

e. "if you're Black"

Part B Directions   Read each sentence. Write _T_ if the statement is true or _F_ if it is not true.

_____ **1.** Nikki Giovanni has devoted much of her career to helping other African-American writers find their way into the spotlight.

_____ **2.** In her poem, she says that she was happy while growing up Black.

_____ **3.** She wants a white author to write a biography about her life.

_____ **4.** The rhyme scheme for this poem is a b c d e f f e

_____ **5.** The setting for this poem is Woodland, a mainly African-American suburb of Cincinnati, Ohio.

Chicago

Directions   Each sentence has one missing word, term, date, or proper name. Below each are three words, terms, dates, or proper names. One of these completes the sentence. Circle the letter of the word, term, date, or proper name that completes the sentence.

1. Carl Sandburg was born in _____.

   a. 1778   **b.** 1878   **c.** 1978

2. Carl Sandburg first earned national attention as a _____ when *Poetry* magazine published "Chicago."

   a. hog butcher   **b.** tool maker   **c.** poet

3. In his work, Sandburg tried to capture the special ways of talking and thinking found in America's _____.

   a. Midwest   **b.** South   **c.** West Coast

4. In the poem "Chicago," Sandburg uses _____, which is the giving of human characteristics to something like a city.

   a. rhyme scheme   **b.** personification   **c.** simile

5. The words *lamp luring* are an example of _____ or the repetition of a beginning sound or letter.

   a. alliteration   **b.** personification   **c.** onomatopoeia

6. The words *tall bold slugger* are an example of _____.

   a. onomatopoeia   **b.** alliteration   **c.** figurative language

7. Toward the poem's end, Sandburg tells us that the city of Chicago is _____.

   a. dying   **b.** laughing   **c.** rising

8. Sandburg's _____, or attitude, toward Chicago is one of admiration and enthusiasm.

   a. tone   **b.** personification   **c.** imagery

9. The _____ of the poem, or the feeling created by the words, is one of vibrant life and action.

   a. repetition   **b.** simile   **c.** mood

10. Sandburg says that some people have told him that Chicago is "_____"; but he loves this city with its "lifted head singing so proud."

    a. too big   **b.** wicked   **c.** wealthy

Unit 7 Review

Part A Directions   Match the writer's tools in Column A with examples of them from Column B. Use each example in Column B only once. Write the letter of the correct answer on the line.

Column A

_____ **1.** alliteration

_____ **2.** assonance

_____ **3.** hyperbole

_____ **4.** imagery

_____ **5.** metaphor

_____ **6.** onomatopoeia

_____ **7.** repetition

_____ **8.** end rhyme

_____ **9.** internal rhyme

_____ **10.** simile

Column B

a. "O, my luve's like a red, red rose,"

b. "Silver bells! . . . How they tinkle, tinkle, tinkle in the icy air of night!"

c. "Be the caller, the called,/The singer, the song, and the sung."

d. "Mother dear, may I go downtown/Instead of out to play,/And march the streets of Birmingham/In a Freedom March today?"

e. "Life is a broken-winged bird"

f. "He left it dead, and with its head"

g. "And I will luve thee still, my dear,/Till a' the seas gang dry."

h. "We real cool. We/Left school."

i. "December. Frost crackling/Beneath my steps,"

j. "this morning/this morning/i met myself"

Unit 7 Review, continued

Part B Directions   Read the lines of poetry. Note the two columns headed
"Poet" and "Poem." In the "Poet" column write the letter from
Column C of the poet who wrote the lines of poetry. In the
"Poem" column, write the letter from Column D of the poem
the lines of poetry are from.

Poet	Poem		Lines of Poetry
_____	_____	**1.**	"She clawed through bits of glass and brick, Then lifted out a shoe."
_____	_____	**2.**	"'Twas brillig, and the slithy toves Did gyre and gimble in the wabe;"
_____	_____	**3.**	"The first time I walked With a girl, I was twelve, Cold, and weighted down With two oranges in my jacket."
_____	_____	**4.**	"Hold fast to dreams For if dreams die Life is a broken-winged bird That cannot fly."
_____	_____	**5.**	"For we all loved our comrade, so brave, young, and handsome, We all loved our comrade, although he'd done wrong.

Column C

a. Lewis Carroll

b. Langston Hughes

c. Dudley Randall

d. Gary Soto

e. Poet Unknown

Column D

f. "Ballad of Birmingham"

g. "Dreams"

h. "Oranges"

i. "The Streets of Laredo"

j. "Jabberwocky"

About Drama

Directions Use the words, terms, and proper name in the Word Bank to complete each set of sentences below.

Word Bank

act	characters	drama	outcome	stage
actions	comedies	flat	playwrights	thoughts
antagonist	dialogue	Greece	protagonist	tragedies

1. Drama is a form of storytelling meant to be performed by actors on a _____. In the Western world, the kinds of drama we see today began in ancient _____.

2. Then and now, _____, or writers of plays, tell stories. They tell them completely through the words and actions of _____.

3. We call some plays _____ because they end unhappily. We call other plays _____ because they have happy endings and are written to amuse people.

4. A _____ is meant to be performed as well as read. It comes from a Greek word that means to do, or to _____.

5. Plays are written to tell a story completely through the words—called _____—of the characters. We also learn the story from the _____ of the characters.

6. The play's main character is the _____. There is usually an _____ who tries to make things difficult for the play's main character.

7. As in all literature, characters in a play can be _____ or round, unchanging or changing. Writers of plays cannot present characters' _____ as can writers of fiction.

8. Plays are divided into two groups according to the _____ of their plots. Some end happily; others end tragically.

Romeo and Juliet

Part A Directions Match each character in Column A with the lines in Column B that he or she spoke in the play. Write the letter of the correct answer on the line.

Column A

_____ **1.** Friar Lawrence

_____ **2.** Juliet

_____ **3.** Paris

_____ **4.** Prince of Verona

_____ **5.** Romeo

Column B

a. "Condemnèd villain, I do apprehend thee./Obey, and go with me; for thou must die."

b. "Romeo, there dead, was husband to that Juliet;/And she, there dead, that's Romeo's faithful wife./I married them;"

c. "For never was a story of more woe/Than this of Juliet and her Romeo."

d. "How fares my Juliet? That I ask again,/For nothing can be ill if she be well."

e. "What's here? A cup, closed in my truelove's hand?/Poison, I see, hath been his timeless end./O churl! Drunk all, and left no friendly drop to help me after? I will kiss thy lips."

Romeo and Juliet, continued

Part B Directions   Place each event in its correct order. Write the letter of the first event from Act V of *Romeo and Juliet* after #1. Write the letter of the second event from the story after #2 and so on. Note that #10 will be the last event.

Events in Order

#1. _____

#2. _____

#3. _____

#4. _____

#5. _____

#6. _____

#7. _____

#8. _____

#9. _____

#10. _____

List of Events to Be Put in Order

a. Paris goes to Juliet's tomb, puts flowers there, and sees Romeo.

b. Juliet wakes from sleep and sees that Romeo is dead.

c. While in Mantua, Romeo has a dream about Juliet, wakes, and feels great joy in their love.

d. The Prince of Verona comes and tells the Capulets and Montagues that they have caused these deaths.

e. Romeo and Paris fight and Romeo kills Paris.

f. Juliet stabs herself with Romeo's knife.

g. Romeo's servant, Balthasar, arrives in Mantua and tells Romeo that Juliet is dead.

h. Romeo drinks poison and dies.

i. The chief watchman comes; finds Romeo and Juliet dead; and sends for the Prince, the Capulets, and the Montagues.

j. Romeo buys some poison from an apothecary in Mantua.

A Raisin in the Sun

Part A Directions   Complete the crossword puzzle by using the fifteen words in the Word Bank.

Across

5. The playwright of this play was the first _____-American woman to have a play produced on Broadway.
7. _____ is the name of the character whose dream is deferred.
8. The last name of the playwright is _____.
10. _____ is the name of the child in the play.
11. The poet Langston Hughes asks "What happens to a _____ deferred?"
13. The playwright who wrote *A Raisin in the Sun* died of _____ at age 34.
14. She was born in _____ in 1930.

Down

1. This play began the career of noted actor and director _____ Poitier.
2. The first name of the playwright is _____.
3. _____ is the character who is getting an insurance check.
4. _____ is the name of the character who wants to be a doctor.
6. _____ Hughes is the poet who asks about deferred dreams.
9. This play was produced on _____.
11. This play won the New York _____ Critics Circle Award for Best Play.
12. _____ is the character married to Walter

Word Bank

African	Mama
Beneatha	Langston
Broadway	Lorraine
cancer	Ruth
Chicago	Sidney
Drama	Travis
dream	Walter
Hansberry	

A Raisin in the Sun, continued

Part B Directions   Match the sentence beginnings in Column A from the play with the sentence endings in Column B from the play. By doing this, create the actual dialogue of the play. Write the letter of the correct answer on the line.

Column A

_____ **1.** "Ain't nothing the matter with me."/

_____ **2.** "There you are. Man say to his woman: I got me a dream."/

_____ **3.** "Now that's your money. It ain't got nothing to do with me."/

_____ **4.** "Been thinking that we maybe could meet the notes on a little old two-story somewhere,"/

_____ **5.** "Mama, you don't understand. It's all a matter of ideas,"/

Column B

a. "His woman say: Eat your eggs."

b. "and God is just one idea I don't accept. It's not important."

c. "We all feel like that—Walter and Bennie and me—even Travis."

d. "with a yard where Travis could play in the summertime, if we use part of the insurance for a down payment and everybody kind of pitch in."

e. "And don't keep asking me that this morning."

Writer's Realm

Directions   Write *True* if the statement is true; write *False* if the statement is not true. Write your answers on the lines provided before each statement. Make each false statement true by drawing a line through its underlined word. Then write the correct word below the statement.

_____   **1.** <u>Anne</u> Jarrell-France has been a television writer, producer, and director.

_____

_____   **2.** In "Writer's Realm," the playwright images that <u>Helen</u> Shelley is discussing her novel with her husband.

_____

_____   **3.** The name of Shelley's science-fiction novel is <u>*Batman*</u>.

_____

_____   **4.** Shelley wrote this novel in the <u>twentieth</u> century.

_____

_____   **5.** In the television script, Shelley first calls the laboratory assistant <u>Bertie</u>.

_____

_____   **6.** On the advice of her husband, she changes the assistant's name to <u>Frankenstein</u>.

_____

_____   **7.** In the television script, Shelley first uses the name Dr. <u>Quimbly-Smythe</u> for the man who makes the monster.

_____

_____   **8.** According to the television script, Shelley first had the doctor create the monster out of plaster and <u>glue</u>.

_____

_____   **9.** Later, according to the script, she decides to have the doctor create the monster out of <u>body</u> parts.

_____

_____   **10.** The doctor uses <u>thunder</u> to bring the monster to life.

_____

Unit 8 Review

Part A Directions   Match each character in Column A with the line or lines in Column B that he or she spoke in one of the three plays. Write the letter of the correct answer on the line.

Column A

_____ **1.** Romeo

_____ **2.** Balthasar

_____ **3.** Apothecary

_____ **4.** Paris

_____ **5.** Friar Lawrence

_____ **6.** Juliet

_____ **7.** Chief Watchman

_____ **8.** Prince of Verona

_____ **9.** Ruth

_____ **10.** Travis

_____ **11.** Walter

_____ **12.** Beneatha

_____ **13.** Mama

_____ **14.** Mary Shelley

_____ **15.** Percy Shelley

Column B

a. "Quite, but don't you think another name would be more appropriate . . . something to go along with the Igor character?"

b. "Go, tell the Prince; run to the Capulets;/Raise up the Montagues; some others search."

c. "O true apothecary!/Thy drugs are quick. Thus with a kiss I die."

d. "No—I'm just sleepy as the devil. What kind of eggs you want?"

e. " . . . Maybe I should give him a more exotic name . . . Igor— what about Igor?"

f. "I *have* to—she won't gimme the fifty cents . . ."

g. "I saw her laid low in her kindred's vault/And presently took post to tell it you."

h. "I'm thirty-five years old: I been married eleven years and I got a boy who sleeps in the living room—and all I got to give him is stories about how rich white people live . . ."

i. "Sweet flower, with flowers thy bridal bed I strew."

j. "Walter, give up; leave me alone—it's Mama's money."

k. "Friar John, go hence,/Get me an iron crow and bring it straight/Unto my cell."

l. "And I, for winking at your discords too,/Have lost a brace of kinsmen. All are punished."

m. "O comfortable friar! Where is my lord?/I do remember well where I should be,/And there I am. Where is my Romeo?"

n. "Now—you say after me, in my mother's house there is still God."

o. "Put this in any liquid thing you will/And drink it off, and if you had the strength/Of twenty men, it would dispatch you straight."

Unit 8 Review, continued

Part B Directions   Read each sentence. Write *T* if the statement is true or *F* if it is not true.

_____ **1.** At the end of *Romeo and Juliet* the two main characters are dead.

_____ **2.** At the end of Act 1, Scene One of *A Raisin in the Sun*, Ruth walks out of the house and leaves her family behind.

_____ **3.** At the end of the television script "Writer's Realm," Mary Shelley decides to name her doctor Frankenstein.

_____ **4.** Shakespeare was born in Stratford-upon-Avon in England.

_____ **5.** Lorraine Hansberry was an American Indian born in Chicago.